FORMULA V

Leading With Vitality

Dr. Richard Kranzley

authorHOUSE®

AuthorHouse™
1663 Liberty Drive
Bloomington, IN 47403
www.authorhouse.com
Phone: 1-800-839-8640

First published by AuthorHouse 11/9/2011

ISBN: 978-1-4567-4569-1 (e)
ISBN: 978-1-4567-4570-7 (dj)
ISBN: 978-1-4567-4571-4 (sc)

Library of Congress Control Number: 2011904241

Printed in the United States of America

TABLE OF CONTENTS

PREFACE

WHACK! Finally it was over. Before the echo of the judge's gavel stopped reverberating off the paneled courtroom walls, Gene felt a surprising calm come over him. A peace he had not felt in years… maybe ever. A peace he had longed for, but had accepted as part of being an executive that he would never truly feel, as long as he was at the helm of the ship of enterprise.

The last two years had been horrific. It began with a subpoena confiscating all of the financial records and communications for the previous five years. He had minimized concerns as well as he could, at the time. The FCC had threatened before, had searched before, finding little. There were relatively minimal fines, but never any charges. This time would be different.

Gene was counting on the fact that everyone had two sets of books; one for the stockholders and one for himself. Everyone, like him, would always tell the truth, but never tell the whole truth. This 'business-as-usual' norm yielded his company tremendous growth. Stocks grew rapidly, splitting twice. For five straight years he and his executive team received their seven-figure bonuses.

Life was good. Well, maybe not so much. While business was great, home life wasn't. His teenage son had left two years ago, accusing him of wreaking his life. His daughter moved in with her boyfriend of two months and vowed never to speak to him ever again. Their mother, his second wife, was filling for divorce, claiming 'irreconcilable differences'.

His family had gotten tired of the hate mail weekly after he closed a plant that had operated in a small town for over 125 years. He closed it to balance the budget in order to cover another bad investment. They were worn out with the picketing outside their home and the constant barrage of reporters who dogged them like they were pop stars, but screaming questions, and sometimes obscenities, about how hazardous waste had gotten into the underground water system down stream from another plant, killing livestock. Investigation was now underway to determine if it had reached the water treatment plant.

It had gotten worse. His former administrative assistant, had thrown him under the proverbial bus. She was also filing a sexual harassment suit and coming out with a tell-all book, not only disclosing questionable deals that were made behind closed doors, but private conversations among competitors to fix a more 'favorable price' for all concerned. The book would also tell of their short three-month affair, ending after pregnancy and an abortion. He had hoped the relationship would help him escape from the pressure he was feeling at work and at home. He had a balanced work life, alright. It was a balanced disaster!

Peace... it was momentarily interrupted when the bailiff pulled on his arm to take him back to his cell, awaiting transport to the minimum security prison where he had just been sentenced for the next twenty years. More peace was to come. A lot of time for peace was coming.

The alarm went off; the same time it had gone off every morning, six days a week at 5:00 am. He was sweating, again, after another restless night. He reached over to touch his wife, to assure himself that the dream was over, at least for this night. How many more nights must he endure this reoccurring nightmare? He didn't know. It was time to get to work; to be the leader of a multi-billion dollar enterprise; to be the leader everyone expected him to be.

There is a charade characteristic in many leaders who have become disconnected from their soul, their core values, maybe not with the dramatic consequences of Gene and his nightmares, but similarly disruptive. It is the daily experience of dissonance between what you believe to be the right thing to do, or what life is calling you to be, and the reality that you are playing out in your daily life.

The result of this disconnection between authenticity and the façade is personal suffering. Over my three decades of consulting and coaching, I have seen it vividly in the lives of leaders who desperately want to find peace in their lives, but who find anything but peace. The consequences are painful: broken relationships, substance abuse, health issues, psychological breakdowns, not to mention the consequences these leaders exert on others including colleagues, stakeholders, employees, vendors, customers, the community, and even family.

I believe this suffering is preventable. I believe that the peace sought is attainable, because the capacity resides within us. I believe if leaders find the peace they seek, we will not fall victim to their betrayal of our trust.

> **"We are not human beings on a spiritual journey, but spiritual beings on a human journey."**
> *Teilhard de Chardin*

If you accept this premise, and I certainly do, then this opens up a fundamental insight of why leadership routinely fails us AND the prescription for how it can reclaim its integrity and thus its significance. After all is said and done, it is one's spirituality that informs and fuels the characteristics or virtues of significant leadership. The degree that one is connected to his/her spirituality will determine the degree to which leadership significance can be achieved.

> **"We're not human beings that have occasional spiritual experiences – it's the other way around: we're spiritual beings that have occasional human experiences."**
> *Deepak Chopra*

Mark Strom, author of <u>The Seven Heavenly Virtues of Leadership</u>, says, "Leading is like bricklaying. We learn to set a string line and work the level. But it's the eye that grows to know what's plumb and true – the art of leadership."

He continues, "Then, there's the mortar, the 'mud'….. Bricklayers don't skimp on mud. They don't measure it out. They throw it on. Extravagantly." Mortar or mud = spirituality! = significance!

> *To the degree one is connected to his/her spirituality will be the degree to which significance can be achieved!*

It isn't a matter of discovery. It is a matter of awareness. Everyone possesses spirituality. Not everyone CHOOSES to connect with his or hers, but everyone has been born with that which connects us all and has been nurtured, to varying degrees, in spiritual environments.

It is important to note that 72% of the world's population, 4.6 billion people out of a total world population of 6.4 billion in 2004, are members and practitioners of the belief and value systems of the Jewish, Christian, Islamic, Hindu or Buddhist religions. If we assume that a similar ratio of religious believers to nonbeliever sexists for employees in organizations, then we have grounds to believe that the topic of spiritual leadership is far more salient to organizational leadership research than is currently understood and acknowledged by organizational researchers. If we are to understand the overall determinants of effective leadership behavior in organizations, it is incumbent upon us to understand the beliefs, values, and paradigms that influence our thinking and behavior.

How many leaders do you know who are in touch with their spirituality, that core which enlivens them and opens them to a world beyond themselves? I am not talking about their religion; I am not talking about their attending church, synagogue, temple, or mosque. I

> *A root cause of leadership failure is the loss of connection with one's spirituality (and its requisite values and virtues).*

am talking about being in touch with their core being, and the virtues and values inherent within that core.

I believe I know your answer because you have experienced the consequences.

So we need to change how we look at leadership. We need a different way to assess men and women for leadership responsibility, focusing first on the qualities, the virtues that are essential for significance, for greatness. Then we might change how we select, promote, mentor, coach, and encourage people with the right qualities.

For this purpose I want to challenge you to think about those virtues or qualities. Where do they come from? What distinguishes leaders with vitality? How might you become one?

And maybe, just maybe, we can cure that Gene-like insomnia you may be experiencing!

INTRODUCTION

So, is this just another book on leadership, one of those self-promoting ones that publishers currently reject, readers ignore, but authors still write?

And, you are asking yourself, why should I read another book on leadership?

Let's take that even one further step... I ask myself, "Why should I write another book on leadership?"

It would be a safe assumption on my part that you have and are suffering both personally and professionally from the effects of poor leadership. Whether it is financial losses, career derailing, abusive behavior, or the deeper suffering of frustration, cynicism, and hopelessness, it feels awful.

If we can harness the energy that resides within us, connecting with that passion, we can multiply our power to lead. It begins with aligning with your inner core and developing the five qualities of significant leadership.

Personal Suffering

If you are a leader, it would also be safe to assume that you have and are suffering from the consequences of being in a highly responsible position where what you say and what you do impacts peoples' lives and the environment in which they live. Whether it is having to live the lonely life of being on top of an organization, or feeling responsible for the pain you have caused by decision or indecision, or the stress and fear that accompanies being in positions of power, you are still human, and it hurts… whether you want to admit it or not.

I sit with the Genes of the world, executives who share their personal pain in dealing with the consequences of making a poor decision. They lament the conflict that has been caused within their teams, the negative impact on performance, and the loss of their own credibility as leaders, all of which are fall-out and subsequent collateral damage from leadership missteps. These leadership regrets become very personal. What I see often is either a loss of courage or, on the other side of the continuum, overreaction… and every dysfunctional behavior in between.

Developing Leaders

Taking it a step away from personal failure, how about developing others as leaders? Senior leaders are constantly engaged in selection and grooming of others to lead. I listen to the criteria that they are using to promote others to more responsible positions or deciding which candidate

> *Is it a surprise when executives don't get what they want and organizations don't get what they need?*

to hire… and I cringe. They are talking more about skill sets that are required or specific experience they have acquired, and little about leadership qualities. Is it then a surprise when they don't get what they want, and the organization doesn't get what it needs? These same leaders end up feeling like they have to "do it all themselves," having to micromanage leadership decisions in their organization. Why? It's because they can't trust the others on their team to perform as leaders strategically or operationally… even though they themselves played a big role in selecting these underperformers. What's wrong with this picture?

I sit with these same executives after making the hire, and listen while they talk about the pain of making the wrong choices in leadership selection. Some of them will take that burden of ownership for their decision and lament... suffer. Others will take the opposite tactic and make someone else personally responsible, deflecting blame for these errors onto human resource professionals, executive recruiters, corporate politics, etc. "How could *they* have done this to me...?" No matter what the response, a lot of pain is involved in these leadership failures.

I say to myself, "It doesn't have to be this way!"

> **"...the evidence leads me to this sobering conclusion: while no leader can single-handedly build an enduring great company, the wrong leader vested with power can almost single-handedly bring a company down. Choose well."**
> *Jim Collins*

The point is that all of this pain, and much of the failure, could be avoided. I hope to help you gain an understanding about what it really means to be a leader that is enlightening and empowering. I hope to guide you in expanding your definition of leadership to encompass a vision of a *significant leader* **who achieves exceptional results**.

I hope to create a choice that we can make... a choice between being a cynic or an optimist; between being desperate or determined; apathetic or enrolled. Through different eyes, we can move from resignation to hope.

I hurt when I see the victims and feel some of their pain. I ache when I meet highly competent, powerful people who suffer through their mistakes and then freeze in their fear of making another one.

And if that isn't enough motivation, it upsets me deeply when I see a list of leaders that in the same breath includes Jesus Christ or Gandhi alongside Hitler and Stalin, naming them all as great leaders. I say to myself, "There is something seriously wrong with our definition of leadership!"

Is leadership truly and solely about influence and getting others to follow? The key word here is "solely..." because although leadership is about influence, it encompasses so much more.

But most of us who study and care about leadership find that just simplistically defining it will carry us down a slippery slope. While conducting my own research of books and articles for this writing, I found myself getting deeper and deeper into the academic/philosophical slippery slopes of intellectual inquiry. Then, at one point I heard this voice in the back of my mind calling, and even pleading, "Earth to Rick! Earth to Rick!"

I was reminded that the last thing I wanted to write was a theoretical treatise on leadership that might be intellectually stimulating, but irrelevant in application. Nor did I want to write 'another book on leadership' identifying the skills and competencies for success. Obviously, the exercise of learning leadership skills and applying them to selection of leaders hasn't helped many of us make better decisions. And I clearly did not want to write a self-help book along with self assessment questions with 'string-of-pearl' insights.

Rather, I want to engage you, the reader; I want to incite you to shift from an intellectual paradigm or the popular behavioral paradigm of leadership discussion to one that lies at the core of our existence, one that is professional and personal.

I want to entertain you, including fables and stories that illustrate, quotations that punctuate, wisdom from around the world that cultivates, and real examples that facilitate insight and expand understanding.

There has been much written in business publications about the doing and having of leadership, identifying competencies and skills that help one meet the metrics and ROI of being successful. Those measurements include profit margins,

> ...Isn't it bliss?
> Don't you approve?
> One who keeps tearing around,
> One who can't move.
> Where are the clowns?
> Send in the clowns...
>
> Don't you love farce?
> My fault I fear.
> I thought that you'd
> want what I want.
> Sorry, my dear.
> But where are the clowns?
> Quick, send in the clowns.
> Don't bother, they're here...
>
> *"Send In the Clowns"*
> by Stephen Sondheim

market share, increased membership, patient/physician satisfaction scores, and sales volume. I have spent years coaching executives who are the students of these behavioral theories for leadership. I have also spent those same years wondering *if this is all there is* to leadership: skill development and behavioral change. But as I mentioned above, when I see the outcomes, when I see the consequences, even if unintended, of how leadership has betrayed its trust, I realize that there has to be a paradigm shift. I don't find a sector anywhere in our society that is not to some degree reeling from failed leadership in both profit and non-profit organizations.

"The changes he makes in his organization are like an iceberg - lasting, but slow to evolve." That is how a direct report assessed the CEO of a multi-billion dollar financial organization.

The Story of Ron

When you talk to Ron you get the impression that he is a visionary, big-picture leader who can impress you with his knowledge, dropping the most current, popular buzz words found in the bestsellers that line his bookcase. With his wealth of experience, razor-sharp sense for best practices and their implementation, and leadership bench strength, he is a tower of leadership power.

On the surface you observe a leader who delegates responsibilities and lets members of his executive team operate independently of his interference. Below the surface, however, you see another story altogether. If Ron has an idea, he gets one of his executive team to authorize themselves to go off and execute it. If it all works out, great. Everyone shares the spotlight. If it doesn't, or if the initiative results in resistance or political fallout, he disavows any knowledge, letting his exec take the heat. "I didn't know he was doing that!" he'd protest to his board and leadership team. "Why on Earth would he think that would work?!!"

You feel yourself thinking that you've seen a rerun of the old TV commercial as you hear him think, "Give it to Mikey… he'll eat, or do, anything!" The afterthought he has, of course, is, "And he'll be the one to eat the consequences!"

When there is a challenge with one of his leaders, Ron simply reorganizes the structure, changing reporting relationships and letting someone else deal with the problem. And the script gets played over and over again.

It is no wonder that Ron's resume is stacked with accomplishments, but, in actuality, is a resume that hides the truth. It is leaders like Ron who get promoted and recruited to ever-increasing responsibilities. Some escape discovery during a lifetime. Others get found out and suffer the consequences, but not before the organization and its people fall victim. Most such leaders themselves know the real truth and live constantly in the grip of a self-imposed hell, in the grip of fear. And they will do almost anything to avoid being found out. Anything! Send in the clowns? Don't bother, they're here, sadly everywhere.

It becomes personal with me. As a coach to executives, it has occurred to me that, as I narrowly focus my work only on behavioral change, am I not an enabler of the failure? Don't I also bear some of the responsibility for the negative consequences of only using a behavioral model of leadership development?

What I am offering, in this attempt at relevance, is to focus on the **qualities or virtues** of leadership, not its competencies or behaviorally defined skills, but its **character**. I am suggesting that we would be better served if we shifted from an epistemological to an ontological approach to leadership. We could all benefit from switching our focus from *doing* leadership to *BEING* a leader.

For the purposes of our conversations on *being* leaders, I will organize it in the following way:

Chapter 1 '*The cry in the wilderness*' that comes from the pain and suffering of poor leadership decisions, and from all who are impacted by them, which creates the urgency for a paradigm shift. "We don't want this! We need something different!"

In beginning our conversations, we will explore in more depth the too frequent, horrific consequences of failed leadership. Thinking this through will leave us with little doubt that we need to do a better job identifying leaders before they assume the role. And once in those roles, we as leaders need to remain connected to our values and those virtues which make us worthy to serve as leaders.

Chapter 2 creates a working definition of leadership, distinguishing between managing and leading, but more importantly, defining leadership that *sustains significant results.*

Chapter 3 returns to the cyclical debate on whether one is born a leader or can be developed as one. I will tell you upfront, the answer is both. BUT I will argue that *only in possessing all the five virtues can one be expected to be a leader for significance.* To state it in colloquial form, you can't make a silk purse out of a sow's ear. In the same vein, you can't be a leader of significance without possessing all of the core qualities to a significant degree. In other words, one can be a leader and develop into a better leader, but only with the core virtues can a leader be significantly great.

Chapters 4 - 8 identify the core qualities or virtues for leadership significance including: **Courage, Humility, Honesty, Altruism, and Resonance.** My practice and research has led me to crystallize these characteristics as those that separate those who are DOING leadership from those who are BEING leaders.

> **"Leadership is a potent combination of strategy and character. But if you must be without one, be without a strategy."**
>
> *General H. Norman Schwarzkopf*

Chapter 9 at this juncture we will delve deeply into the essence of leadership, the thread that turbo-charges the qualities toward significance and brings vitality. Our conversations about the character of leadership now moves us away from the superficial focus on behavior, and takes us to a deeper place, to the heart of significant leadership. This heart is leading with one's spirit. *Spirit* is "a sense of profound connection to things beyond or within one's own self." Spirituality is the heart and soul of leadership. Spirituality (not religion) is an often ignored/denied energy that crosses the boundaries of culture and faith, defining who we are and how we act. Our unique, individual spirit defines the action and reaction, the sum of behavior, which characterizes each of us.

Chapter 10 explores the structure for BEING a leader (rather than doing leading); the disciplines, the routines that significant leaders have practiced that have helped them BE what life is calling them to be as leaders.

The field of leadership has struggled to understand what exactly leadership is, under what contexts or situations it is effectively exercised, and how to explain leadership processes, in addition to leader traits, skills and competencies. As we read about both current events and even events of history, it becomes apparent that the defining spirit of a leader can move him or her down a path of construction or destruction.

In our world today, we are further challenged by an increasingly uncertain and rapidly evolving global economy where leadership is affected by not only the values of national cultures, but also the belief systems and paradigms of the world's varying religious traditions. It becomes paramount for a leader in today's world to understand his or her own spirit and how that core of being and connection will equate to leadership significance for today... and for tomorrow.

One final note: Don't expect me to lift up examples of leaders who exemplify being a Leader for Significance. If I did, we would get bogged down, hijacked in a debate about *who* rather than a preferred dialogue about *what*. As we explore together the virtues of significant leadership, you will naturally find examples from your own experience and wisdom that will illustrate leadership success and failure. After all, it is that analysis of self and others that I hope will become part of your thought and learning process.

CHAPTER I

LOOKING FOR LEADERSHIP
In All the Wrong Places...And in the Wrong People

> **Significance**: *a quality or aspect having great worth. Implies importance because of probable or possible effects.*

Aristotle warned of **hubris**, or *pride/excessive ambition,* as the great downfall of great men; Shakespeare wrote tragedies in which protagonists were ruined via this overriding character flaw. In the last decade, America has been living its own Greek tragedy, where a small group of the powerful, spurred by their excessive pride and greed, have managed to unsettle the entire U. S. banking system, not to mention creating world-wide financial instability.

From the moment humans are born, we turn to those in authority to provide answers, comfort, sustenance, and safety. Our first concern as newborns is to find the milk supply, and then to figure out how to keep it flowing. Babies do whatever is necessary to make that happen: laugh, cry, smile, or whine. As with other mammals, this dependence on authority is hardwired into our human DNA. Teenagers develop more complex and nuanced relationships with parents, teachers, coaches, and other authority figures. But even rebellious teenagers and otherwise self-sufficient adults often look again to authorities to provide direction, protection, and order when problems arise (Heifetz, Grashow, Linsky, 2009).

Leaders and Followers – a Codependency

There is a codependency here: humans need leaders and leaders need followers. This symbiosis works as long as each meets the needs of the other. But when one or the other does not meet expectations, the 'dark side' of our human nature raises its ugly head. You and I have been there, and we have experienced its ugliness.

Leadership has dishonored its sacred trust. Through its *arrogance* it has ignored the collective wisdom. Through its *indifference* it has become immune to the ramifications and consequences of its behavior. Through its *cowardice* it has shied away from doing the right thing. Through its *selfishness* it has disrespected humanity.

> *Leadership has dishonored its sacred trust.*

Highly publicized failures of corporate leadership in as widely disparate organizations as Enron, WorldCom, Tyco, Arthur Andersen, and the Roman Catholic Church in the United States have dramatically harmed the lives of tens of thousands of persons inside and outside these institutions. At the same time, the public at large is left with deeply shaken confidence in our institutions and those who lead them. A shadow is cast over the promise of our future.

We are in crisis. But this state of crisis is nothing new. Leaders have risen from the ranks only to support the Peter Principle. Individuals have assumed the mantle of the sacred trust of leadership, only to be found out later to be frauds. We have leader-clones who are trained in best practices and styles of others which masks conformity, rather than value based originality!

"For too long we have been training leaders who only know how to keep the routine going. Who can answer questions, but don't know how to ask them. Who can fulfill goals, but don't know how to set them. Who think about how to get things done, but not whether they're worth doing in the first place… What we don't have are leaders" (Deresiewicz, 2010).

In our organizations today across all sectors, individuals and search committees are being asked to find strong leadership. Their task, once challenging, has become monumental in the shadows of recent history. The search for leadership might have trouble defining this 'something', but hopefully it will be recognized when it is seen… that knack for inspiring trust, perhaps, or a talent for creating enthusiasm for change, or the ability to provide a sense of direction in a confusing world. Those in search of leaders might even hope to find someone with a certain charisma who excites and inspires. Or they might find a clone of a successful leader mirroring competency.

But in the end, decisions have too often failed to achieve desired results. Can we expect anything different in the future without changing how we think about leadership?

While we may benefit short term, celebrating ROI successes, we have paid the price for our miscalculation and blind trust. As voters, constituents, senior managers, board members, and other decision makers in leader selection, aren't we also partially to blame?

The Role We Play

After all, we are the ones who chose to promote incompetence through our votes, our acquiescence, and by proxy, through our managers, our recruitment staff, our board members. We are the ones who didn't hold leaders accountable, looking the other way, silent in our outrage while lowering our expectations.

There is always someone who has encouraged the would-be leader. There are others who turn their heads, ignoring the signs of incompetence or questionable intent. There are still others who keep silent in their descent (not to forget those who didn't and lost their lives for it) while the small lies and omissions morph into malice. After all, leadership requires enablers.

What is worse, cynicism has become pervasive and has created an environment where one assumes the leader is lying, greedy, selfish, and untrustworthy. Be it in government or any other private or non-profit organization, with such a climate it can be next to impossible for leaders, even the good ones, to lead in the

> *"All we have to do is make sure we don't put psychotics in high places."* Thomas Wolfe

face of followers' cynicism. At this point the followers have bought into a debauched definition of leadership, and have lost hope.

Leadership requires followership. If the followers won't follow, there is no leadership. This is the greatest tragedy of all, because it undermines the ability for us to escape the consequences of poor leadership and holds us as victims. It doesn't feel good and it is scary.

"All we have to do is make sure we don't put psychotics in high places," Thomas Wolfe promised. But with our indifference or cynicism, haven't we? Won't we?

Conger and Kanungo (1998) argue that most leaders tend to pursue simultaneously both personal and organizational interests. They point to a dark side of leadership, where leaders may have a tendency at times towards narcissism, authoritarianism, Machiavellianism, and a high need for personal power. Many of us only have to look down the hallway in our workplace to see this in action.

Our current crisis of confidence pales in comparison to the horrific consequences of failed leadership that history records. Let's not forget:

Genghis Khan was quite possibly the greatest military leader of all time. He built an empire that stretched from the coast of China to the Black Sea and pushed north into Russia. In size, his conquests exceeded that of both Alexander the Great and Napoleon. But his name became synonymous with cruelty and terror. He butchered millions and trusted no one. Those he let live were burdened with hard work and heavy tribute.

In 25 years, the Mongol army subjugated more lands and people than the Romans had conquered...well over three million people. Whether measured by the total number of people defeated, the sum of the countries annexed, or by the total area occupied, Genghis Khan conquered more than twice as much as any other man in history. The most astonishing aspect of this achievement is that the entire Mongol tribe under Genghis Khan numbered around a million, smaller than the workforce of some modern corporations.

The cost of his leadership? During his reign, 10 million died from genocide, massacres, famine and disease.

Hernando de Soto in his search for gold, was the first European to land in Florida and proceeded to commit full-scale genocide on native peoples. He was a monster, having burned his first man alive in his teens. While murdering and pillaging his way across parts of Central and South America, he acquired skills that would have chilled a Nazi SS officer. A mighty leader who earned his place in history books, municipal parks, auto designs, and roadside markers, despite his despicable behavior. (Gear, 2010)

Adolph Hitler oversaw one of the greatest expansions of industrial production and civil improvement Germany had ever seen. The unemployment rate was cut substantially. There were the largest infrastructure-improvement campaigns in German history, with the construction of dozens of dams, railroads, and other civil works. Hitler's policies emphasized the importance of pre-World War II family life. Men were the breadwinners, while women's priorities were bringing up children and performing household work.

However, it can be said Hitler was the one who was responsible for three of 20th century's most climactic events: 1) World War II; 2) the Holocaust (6 million Jews murdered); and arguably, 3) the Cold War, which followed World War II. The fall-out from World War II kept entire nations – East Germany and many Eastern European countries -under one or another form of repression for decades. Adolf Hitler is regarded as one of the most despicable men in history, with his name becoming synonymous with evil. As the leader of the Third Reich, he can be identified with causing tens of millions of deaths and ruined nations. But he was quite an effective leader.

Joseph Stalin was the unrivalled leader of the Soviet Union, ruling from 1928 until his death in 1953. He modernized the country through Five Year Plans, which consisted of forced collectivization and industrialization. Intentional food shortages became a planned famine known as the Holodomor in the Ukraine. Despite Stalin's harsh rule, the Soviet Union under his leadership became a world power and even acquired a brief technological lead in space exploration. Yet, his leadership brought 1.2 million deaths in a two-year period, during which 100 human beings were killed per day!

These were not isolated incidences, but predictable disasters. And history keeps repeating itself. More recent examples might include:

Idi Amin swept a wide swath of destruction, his victims including members of other ethnic groups, religious leaders, journalists, senior bureaucrats, judges, lawyers, students and intellectuals, criminal suspects, and foreign nationals. Bodies floated on the River Nile in quantities sufficient to clog the Owen Falls Hydro-Electric Dam. One estimate puts those killed at 500,000.

Saddam Hussein presided over an ethnically divided nation, and used his power to hold it together. But in the process he master-minded large-scale deportations, destruction of villages, and executions. Saddam ordered attacks against the country's non-Arab Kurdish population during the 1988 Anfal campaign that rose to the level of genocide.

Slobodan Milosevic became known as the "Butcher of the Balkans." This infamous leader led the killing of 230,000 people, with three million displaced.

What other names will be added to the records of history? Will the list include **Ahmadinejad**, or **Kim Jong-il**? And with the development of technology, are the potential consequences even more unimaginable and more frequent?

Do I overstate the threat of continuing to look for leadership in all the wrong places and in the wrong people? At the risk of distracting us from our main discussion, I have provided you with these albeit disturbing examples to focus on the power of leadership and its attendant consequences if misused. Acknowledging the risks of regrettable choices, we have an opportunity to shape history to prevent repeating our past mistakes.

We must be compelled to reconsider our description of leadership as a simple categorization of traits or skills that lead one to power. When we lump the names of despicable despots in the same category of leadership along with Ghandi, Abraham Lincoln, Jesus Christ, Nehru, Mohammed, and Winston Churchill, we can quickly see that something is wrong with our definition. While they all truly have had great influence in our society, they have done so with quite differing significance; the virtues they possess as leaders differentiate between despots and saints.

> *We have an opportunity to shape history to prevent repeating our past mistakes.*

Do I dare, in the same conversation, include the CEOs, and financial and political leadership that led to the 2008 economic meltdown? This may seem an overreaching stretch. However, the human costs to this recent economic tragedy are enormous. Add to it the crisis in the real estate and lending sectors, and we see millions of families losing their livelihood and pensions, losing their homes and their stability. Some may view the comparison as overly dramatic; but they would not be within the ranks of the homeless created by the failure of leadership in our country today. I would argue that it is the same kind of leadership that enabled the despots of history. It all is leadership without courage, honesty, humility, resonance and altruism. It all is leadership that is not spirited!

God forbid that the world will have to endure another horrible period as a result of tyrannical leadership. By continuing to be cynical or indifferent, we will, in fact, sustain the environment that could enable those who would lead tragically to assume power. After all, it takes followers for leaders to exist.

We need to change our definition of leadership. We need to shift our distinctions and assessments from skills and competencies to qualities and character.

When we confuse qualities with competencies, we run the risk of **choosing** *a leader without character*; a leader who will provide short term successes without long-term impact; a leader with skill, but no heart.

It is too late to undo the damage that has been done. It may be too late for the present generation to reverse the cynicism grown out of our experience with failed leadership. But it is not too late to learn from our mistakes. It is not too late to redefine what we expect from leaders in whom we place our trust. It definitely is time to accept Jim Collins' charge, in his work *Good to Great*, to put together an understanding of leadership that will transform our thinking, re-focus our distinctions around leadership, and direct our behavior and decisions.

This writing is for the parent, educator, business owner, manager, executive board member, cleric - anyone in a position to identify, nurture, direct, and elevate extraordinary character to be realized. Make no mistake, *significant leadership* will always be recognized. What is at stake is to what degree and to what extent will be the influence... and the impact.

And with this in mind, let's answer the question:

What makes significant leaders?

What adjectives would you choose to describe significant leaders?

What definitions and styles would you select for leaders who will make a difference, a positive difference in people's lives?

Is there a formula for leading with vitality, for significant results?

Chapter 2

'SIGNIFICANT LEADERSHIP'
A Definition

> Time Magazine solicited nominees for 'great leaders' from a wide variety of people, politicians, philosophers, clerics, etc. Depending on one's orientation, and nationality, historical perspective, the list is quite diverse, some known better than others... all labeled by some as 'great leaders.' The list of nominees included:
>
> Genghis Khan, Alexander the Great, Frederick II of Prussia, Napoleon, Winston Churchill, Thomas Jefferson, James Madison, George Washington, Abraham Lincoln, Franklin D. Roosevelt, Woodrow Wilson, Shah of Iran, Swedish Prime Minister Olaf Palme, Marlborough, Wellington, Adolph Hitler, Al Capone, Julius Caesar, Lorenzo de' Medici, Camillo Benso di Cavour, George Marshall, Charles de Gaulle, Mohammed, Jesus Christ, Buddha, Lenin, Mao, John F. Kennedy, Martin Luther King, Gandhi and Nehru, Moses, Konrad Adenauer, Pasteur, Salk, Confucius, Sigmund Freud, Karl Marx, Epicurus, and Kao-Tsu. (TIME, July, 1974)

This list will certainly raise questions in your mind about 'what must they be thinking to include....' This list will naturally make you question why this or that person was not included. I find it disturbing that my top names of greatness have been included, along with those I would identify with evil.

My upset simply drives my resolve toward relevant distinctions and clearer definitions.

Perhaps it would be helpful to think of leadership as a field of study, filled with definitions, theories, styles, functions, competencies, and historical examples of successful though diverse

> *I find it disturbing that my top names of greatness have been included, along with those I would identify with evil.*

practitioners. After all, we confuse our understanding by mixing our metaphors, our examples, and, thus, our adjectives.

When we are talking about leadership, are we talking about skills and competencies, or are we talking about characteristics and traits? **These distinctions will influence whether we believe leadership is a learned or innate characteristic; whether it is more important to develop managers or recruit leaders.**

It is too naive to suggest that it is an either/or proposition. Rather, it is a combination. I will argue that we too often lean toward believing leaders are created (terminology = developed/coached), and the subsequent behavior is developed. Too often, we believe that all we need to do is change the behavior of an individual and he/she becomes a leader. It follows that all you have to do to become a leader for significance is to change that much more.

In my experience, everyone has their ceiling of competency, whether they want to admit it or not. When the challenges of the job exceed the ceiling of their leadership, we then see failure and its consequences, even if unintended.

The problem is that this ceiling of competency, and the routine occurrence of the Peter Principle, fly under the radar of our awareness and of those who make the important decisions. Those making the decisions on leadership promotion can be blind to the folly of their choices. "He's been here for 20 years. He knows the business." Or... "He's been in our industry forever. He did a great job for our competitors, so he'll be perfect in this role." Of course, he's the best person for this job. Or… is he?

There has to be another way. The prices we pay have become too great to ignore, try as we might. The paradigm shift required starts with clarity in our definitions and the language we use.

Defining Leadership

There are over 1,983,980 definitions of *leadership and leadership characteristics* on the Internet. Trying to narrow down this widely diverse understanding of what it means to be a leader may be an impossible task. What I have decided to do is to share some of the definitions, distinguishing between confusion of the terms 'managing' and 'leading', ending with a definition that will be utilized throughout this writing, a definition that includes the qualifying adjective, *"significance"*.

Here is a sampling of definitions from the world of business and academia:

> **"A leader is best when people barely know he exists. When his work is done, they will say: we did it ourselves."**
>
> *Lao-Tzu*

> **"Leadership is the ability to get extraordinary achievement from ordinary people."**
>
> *Brian Tracy*

> **"Leadership is the art of getting someone else to do something you want done because he wants to do it."**
>
> *Dwight D. Eisenhower.*

> **"A true leader has the confidence to stand alone, the courage to make tough decisions, and the compassion to listen to the needs of others. He does not set out to be a leader, but**

becomes one by the equality of his actions and the integrity of his intent."

Douglas MacArthur

"There are three essentials to leadership: humility, clarity and courage."

Chan Master Fuchan Yuan

"A leader is a person who is truly effective in achieving worthy results in any field, no matter what the obstacles and with unfailing regard for human beings. A leader is a person of unimpeachable character, and can be trusted. Leaders are open-minded, good listeners, flexible, secure in the knowledge that they alone do not have all the answers."

Peter Koestenbaum

"In Aristotelian terms, the good leader must have ethos, pathos and logos. The ethos is his moral character, the source of his ability to persuade. The pathos is his ability to touch feelings, to move people emotionally. The logos is his ability to give solid reasons for an action, to move people intellectually."

Mortimer Adler

"Leadership has nothing to do with morality. A leader gets people to follow him."

Correlli Barnett

"No concept of leadership is complete without the element of zeal and fervor, an almost spiritual element."

Alexander Heard

"Leaders must fulfill three functions —provide for the well-being of the led, provide a social organization in which people feel relatively secure, and provide them with one set of beliefs."

Jules Masserman

"A great leader has original ideas and succeeds in having them accepted by millions or billions. These ideas can be wonderful or dreadful."

Jean-Francois Revel

"… leadership has no personal greed for power but cares rather for the welfare of the people, using persuasion instead of violence, never allowing expediency to justify a deviation from the truth."

Yu Ying-Shih

One begins to see the threads of qualities of leadership surfacing in these samplings, qualities of courage, charity, compassion, integrity, humility, clarity, and sensitivity. All have the element of influence.

And often we get confused with our defining leadership when we do not distinguish between being a manager and being a leader.

Distinguishing Between Boss and Manager, and Leader

When we begin our careers, we are hired for our technical competency. Getting the work done is the value we bring to the organization (The Employee).

As we progress, so does our value. Added to technical expertise is our supervisory skill, how we enable others to do the work (The Manager). During this period in our careers, to varying degrees, we will divorce ourselves from doing the actual work, but still stay 'in-the-weeds.'

Typically, as our accomplishment grows, we assume more and more responsibilities, making it more and more difficult to actually do the work we were hired to do and valued for early in our career. Then our value shifts from 'managing' to 'leading'. Here you are valued for your strategic, big picture thinking, enrolling people into the vision, and creating an environment to maximize productivity and success (The Leader).

As I work with people trying to make this leap from manager to leader, it is often a difficult and scary bridge to cross. What has made you successful in the past is no longer required of you. There are others to do that work. What is required are other skill sets that may or may not align with your core, natural competencies. You may be thrust into a discomfort zone where you haven't been before. And as we will see in Chapter 4, it conjures up all kinds of feelings and behavior, some good, some not so good.

What helps is to become clear what the differences are between being a manager/boss and being a leader. In making these distinctions, we will create the platform from which we will launch our discovery of the virtues of great leadership. The following is a sampling from the mouths of sages.

> "The boss drives people; the leader coaches them. The boss depends on authority; the leader on goodwill. The boss inspires fear; the leader inspires enthusiasm. The boss says "I"; the leader says "WE". The boss fixes the blame for the breakdown; the leader fixes the breakdown. The boss says "GO"; the leader says 'LET'S GO'!"
>
> *H. Gordon Selfridge*

> "A boss creates fear, a leader confidence. A boss fixes blame, a leader corrects mistakes. A boss knows all, a leader asks questions. A boss makes work drudgery, a leader makes it interesting. A boss is interested in himself/herself, a leader is interested in the group."
>
> *Russell H. Ewing*

> "People ask the difference between a leader and a boss. The leader works in the open, and the boss is covert. The leader leads, and the boss drives."
>
> *Theodore Roosevelt*

> "You manage things; you lead people."
>
> *Rear Admiral Grace Murray Hopper*

"Managers do things right; leaders do the right thing."
Stephen Covey

Warren Bennis (1989) drew 12 distinctions between managers and leaders:

- ➤ Managers administer, leaders innovate
- ➤ Managers ask how and when, leaders ask what and why
- ➤ Managers focus on systems, leaders focus on people
- ➤ Managers do things right, leaders do the right things
- ➤ Managers maintain, leaders develop
- ➤ Managers rely on control, leaders inspire trust
- ➤ Managers have a short-term perspective, leaders have a long-term perspective
- ➤ Managers accept the status quo, leaders challenge the status quo
- ➤ Managers have an eye on the bottom line, leaders have an eye on the horizon
- ➤ Managers imitate, leaders originate
- ➤ Managers emulate the classic good soldier, leaders are their own person
- ➤ Managers copy, leaders show originality

These definitions and distinctions have also been collated into categories of styles, styles of leadership that have evolved over the years. A brief summary of styles will add to our understanding about leadership (if not our confusion of what exactly we are talking about).

Different Leadership Styles

The *laissez-faire*, "leave it be" **leadership** (Lewin, Lippit, White, 1939) is the leadership style that gives no continuous feedback or supervision, because the employees are highly experienced and need little supervision to obtain the expected outcome.

The **bureaucratic leader** (Weber, 1905) is very structured and follows the procedures as they have been established.

The charismatic leader (Weber, 1905) leads by infusing energy and eagerness into the team members.

The Autocratic leader (Lewin, Lippit, White, 1939) has been given the power to make decisions based solely on his person, having total authority.

The democratic leader (Lewin, Lippit, and White, 1939) means that the leader will hear the team's ideas and study them, but will make the final decision.

The people-oriented leader (Fiedler, 1976) is the one that, in order to comply with effectiveness and efficiency, supports, trains and develops his personnel, increasing job satisfaction and genuine interest to do a good job.

Task oriented leaders (Fiedler, 1967) are those who focus on the job and concentrate on the specific task assigned to each employee to reach the goal of competency.

The servant leader (Greenleaf, 1977) is the leader who facilitates goal accomplishment by giving its team members what they need in order to be productive.

The transaction leader (Burns, 1978) leads through power given to a certain person to perform certain tasks, and reward or punish for the team's performance.

The transformation leader (Burns, 1978) is the one who motivates its team to be effective and efficient.

The environment leader (Carmazzi, 2005) is the one who nurtures an environment to affect the emotional and psychological perception of an individual's place in the group or organization.

The situation leader (Joseph Praveen Kumar, Hersey, Blanchard, Johnson, 2008) is the leader who uses different leadership styles depending on the situation and the type of employee that is being supervised.

You and I might conclude from this summary that leadership is many things to many people, or that no one has a clue. It could also mean that it depends on the situation, the environment, and the period of time. It means that there are a wide variety of styles to fit a wide range of needs. But can we draw upon this diversity to simplify our understanding? If so, we can be clear what contributes to the leadership we have defined.

That is why I will attempt to simplify our quest to find meaning and relevance to leadership. I will try to do what has been impossible to do by adding an adjective to leadership that will distinguish it from common terminology and raise the bar of excellence and greatness. When used against the list above, it will quickly separate the wheat from the shaft. The word I would attach to leadership is *SIGNIFICANCE.*

Significance: *having major or important consequence. Quality of having great value. Goes to intent.*

Syn: *WORTH, IMPORTANCE*

Ant: *TRIVIALITY*

Leadership is influential. Leadership is about relationship. It is about influencing that relationship and all the competencies and qualities that go with effective influencing.

The 'Great Man' theory of leadership sought to identify the traits, or distinguishing personal characteristics of effective leaders. Some distinguishing traits identified include energy and stamina, intelligence, optimism, self-confidence, interpersonal skills, and drive to excel. The focus is the <u>observable</u> world that can be directly measured, or inferred, using the scientific method.

Beneath these traits, however, lies the essence of leadership that forms the foundation for the competencies. The quality of leadership is itself influenced by the character of the individual holding the position of leadership.

> ## FORMULA V
> ### Leading with Vitality

Based on my research and experience there are *FIVE qualities* of leadership that predictably will create desirable outcomes, the results of which will be sustained long after the leader is gone and be labeled significant. These qualities have been found to have an effect on leadership success.

The Five Qualities are: **Courage, Humility, Honesty, Resonance, and Altruism**. They are the essence of FORMULA V.

Significant Leadership: *Possessed with courage, humility, honesty, resonance and altruism, the intent to influence others to the degree that leads to valued outcomes, great consequence and lasting effect.*

Debate as we might about what has been included or not, we can begin to understand how important it is to have a fundamental base from which to assess leadership significance and, from that base, to identify its source.

Chapters 4 thru 8 will attempt to define and distinguish each virtue. But first, let's think about how these virtues appear in the first place.

Are the virtues for significant leading born to us, or are they conditioned in us?

Your leadership qualities… did you learn them, or were some of them simply part of who you are?

Chapter 3

LEADERSHIP
Born or Bred?

Story of Andrew – the Natural

He hadn't seen it coming. Surely the financials were not great, but neither were everyone else's. And he always was able to meet the challenge before, it was only a matter of time. But time had run out for Andrew.

He was a 'natural'. Gifted. That is what Andrew's parents, teachers, colleagues and bosses always said. He had 'it': the charisma, intelligence and drive that made for great leadership.

It was obvious very early on in his life. He'd been targeted during fourth grade for that little group, the Leadership Gifted, who got to do cool service projects on Fridays when the rest of the kids were taking their spelling and science tests. And it got better from there. He was elected President of the Student Body, Captain of the football team, on the 'fast track' soon after being hired at his first job, youngest to be promoted to Vice President, and President of the Chamber of Commerce. It seemed that no matter what he did, people naturally turned to him for leadership.

That is why he was having so much difficulty accepting the fact that he had been passed over for the Senior VP position, and instead had been assigned to lead a remote division of the company, jokingly labeled the "Siberia Assignment" – where the failures were sentenced for the rest of their career with the company.

He always relied on his gifts. That is why, when moved to rescue a troubled division, he thought nothing of it, believing his own press releases: "a natural at turnarounds." And why not believe it? He had been able to do it in the past.

He'd been given some tips by a couple of the older guys in the division, but he hadn't needed their input. It flew in the face of his success at his previous company, where he'd led them to a terrific finish in a race with the competition. That is why he ignored the advice to take a more measured, deliberate approach to the necessary changes, rather than the typical taking-the-hill-by-storm.

That is why he didn't spend the recommended time with the current leadership of the division to enroll them into his vision. In the past, everyone would always come around and follow. After all, he was their leader. Isn't that what they were paying him the big bucks to do?

Andrew relied on what came naturally to him, what was in his comfort zone. When the internal conflict arose, the press got hold of the latest earnings reports. He became a victim of the "If-It-Ain't-Broke-Don't-Fix-It" dream world where he never saw beyond what was easy for him.

Yes, he had started with an advantage. He'd had the right stuff from the beginning. But in the glow of his success complacency set in. Andrew never sought to grow and develop into someone better, greater, because he already possessed 'it.' It was a façade he hid behind until it was too late.

He believed that you were born to be a leader. He was... and he wasn't.

Is leadership an innate ability or a developed competency? It is an old debate with a new reality.

BORN A. K. A. NATURE

It seems as though we hear almost daily of a new genetic discovery. Genes are now linked to Alzheimer's disease, bedwetting, obesity, and even to overall happiness. Many aspects of development that were previously attributed to learning, bad habits, or environment are now thought to be determined by our genes.

It's hard to explain child prodigies, young children who can play piano or chess at master level, or can paint gallery-quality art works with little or no instruction. Given the lack of training/practice/learning involved when such a child can perform these amazing feats at the ages of 3 or 4 years – or even by the age of 7 – we can easily see that these incredibly gifted individuals must possess an inborn talent. That would mean that they have been born with innate abilities, with one or a combination of genes for the intellectual and physical capabilities that they demonstrate through their marvelous performances.

The Twinning Effect

Taking our look at heredity in another way, the remarkable twinning effect reinforces the notion of the importance of heredity in some abilities. Research on identical twins raised in very different environments supports the strength of the premise of inborn wiring, and it directly contradicts the notion that environment is more important than genes. In some of these cases, twins who were raised apart with no contact, and are reunited years later, find that their lives are very similar. Their choice of hairstyles, clothing, mannerisms, chosen occupations and other variables may mirror each other in an uncanny way – again, even though they didn't even know each other during their childhood years.

This was the case of a pair of twin brothers separated five weeks after birth and raised 80 miles apart in Ohio. When Jim Lewis and Jim Springer were reunited at the age of 39, they found they both married women named Linda, divorced, and remarried women named Betty. Both chain-smoked Salem cigarettes, drank Miller light, loved stock car racing, hated baseball, and vacationed on the same stretch of beach in

Florida. Go figure! This is just one example, and there are hundreds - if not thousands - of twin studies that give us similar results.

However, we humans are complex creatures, and we are not merely prisoners of either our genes or our environment. We have free will. Genes are overruled every time an angry man restrains his temper, a fat man diets, or an alcoholic refuses to take a drink.

BRED A. K. A. NURTURE

Many successful leaders feel their success is conditioned into them. They feel their confidence is learned from experience, since it increases over time as they achieve more success. When a successful leader is young, he often feels trepidation in front of more senior people, or when confronted with difficult situations; yet, he later becomes more confident. So, it must be learned, right?

Popular wisdom today would have us believe that *it is nonsense to assume that leadership is genetic. There is no hard evidence to support that assumption, and worse, it dooms every one of us to accept our limitations as our destiny.*

The truth is that leadership is an observable set of skills and abilities that are useful, whether one is in the executive suites or on the front line, on Wall Street or Main Street. And any skill can be strengthened and enhanced, if we have the motivation and desire, the practice and feedback, the role models and coaching, and the support and recognition.

Of course, this is an excerpt from an advertisement for a leadership development organization (thus, the quotation marks). But there are many followers of this position.

- **"Leaders aren't born, they are made and they are made just like anything else, through hard work, and that's the price we will have to pay to achieve that goal, or any goal"** (Vince Lombardi).

- "The most dangerous leadership myth is that leaders are born, that there is a genetic factor to leadership.... The myth asserts that people simply either have certain charismatic qualities or not. That's nonsense; in fact, the opposite is true. Leaders are made, rather than born" (Warren G. Bennis).

- "I believe that there are natural drives and preferences that add some credibility to the idea that leaders are born. It has been shown that from the early stages of life some individuals strive for control and expression; and others do not." (Joseph Currier). Currier calls this the Executive Factor. The "E-factor" is a neuropsychologically determined propensity to lead, a natural drive.

Leadership is nutured. But on the other hand, the environment is overruled every time a genetic defect wins out, as when Lou Gehrig's athletic ability was overruled by his ALS. Genes and environment work together to shape our brains, and we can manage them both if we want to do so. It may be harder for people with certain genes or surroundings, but level of difficulty in achieving leadership success is still a long way from taking a purely hard-wired, predetermined view of leadership ability.

> *It is biologically impossible for a gene to operate independently of its environment.*

It is biologically impossible for a gene to operate independently of its environment. Genes are designed to be regulated by signals from their immediate surroundings, including hormones from the endocrine system and neurotransmitters in the brain, some of which, in turn, are profoundly influenced by our social interactions. Just as our diet can regulate certain genes, our social experiences and learning can also determine a distinctive batch of such genomic off-on switches.

Our genes, then, are not sufficient in themselves to produce an optimally operating nervous system. Raising a secure child, or an empathetic one, in this view, requires not just a necessary set of genes, but also sufficient parenting or other reinforcing social experiences. Only this combination ensures that the right genes will operate in the best way.

Thus, with all the determinism built into the initial wiring of our brain, experience with our surrounding environment refines and, in some cases, rewires that initial wiring.

THE BALANCE BETWEEN NATURE AND NURTURE

Recent research at the University of Minnesota indicates that about 35% to 50% of the characteristics we associate with leadership may come from genes. For example, their findings include genetic advantages such as: impressive appearance, energetic behavior, good speaking abilities, having an empathetic manner.

But nurturance also plays a role. Psychologist Manfred de Vries has noted that great leaders often have absent fathers and strong mothers. He includes examples such as Alexander the Great, George Washington, Winston Churchill, and Douglas MacArthur.

Michael Meaney has discovered, at least for mice, a vital way that parenting can change the very chemistry of a youngster's genes. His research identifies a singular window in development, the first 12 hours after a rodent's birth, during which a crucial mental process occurs. How much a mother rat licks and grooms her pups during this window actually determines how brain chemicals that respond to stress will be made in that rat pup's brain for the rest of its life (Meaney, 2001). That could explain why your hated leader is such a rat!

The more nurturing the mother is, the more quick witted, confident, and fearless the pup will become; and conversely, the less nurturing she is, the slower to learn and more overwhelmed by threats her pup will be. Just as telling, the mother's level of licking and grooming determines how much a female pup, in turn, will lick and groom her own pups one day. So, the mother's behavior will affect not only her immediate litter, but also many litters (or generations) to come.

The human equivalents of licking and grooming seem to be empathy, nurturance, and touch. If Meaney's work translates to humans, as he suspects it does, then how our parents treated us has left its genetic imprint over and above the set of DNA they passed down to us. Extrapolating further, how we treat our children will, in turn, set levels of activity in their genes. This finding suggests that small, caring acts of parenthood can matter in lasting ways, and that relationships have a hand in guiding the brain's continuing redesign.

Jack Welch, former CEO of GE, wrote a book about his experiences running a large corporation. He says he is often asked whether leadership can be learned, or whether it comes as part of the 'package' (innate). His answer is: "a little bit of both." He agrees that IQ and energy level are probably innate, but that self-confidence is learned "at your mother's knee."

A mere 50,000 genes for the brain are not nearly enough to account for the hundred trillion synaptic connections that are made there. Genes set boundaries for human behavior; but within these boundaries there is opportunity for variation determined by experience, personal choice, and even chance.

Most of our traits are caused by the interaction of many genes as influenced by the environment. Environment can even negate strong genetic predispositions.

Studies of 7,000 sets of twins by the Minnesota Center for Twin and Adoption Research showed any number of traits may be driven by genes, including alienation, **leadership**, vulnerability to stress, and even religious conviction and career choice.

Other twin studies show that environment can mitigate or exaggerate the effect of genes. Twin halves raised by parents living in a tough inner-city environment demonstrate more aggressive and violent behavior than the other twin halves raised in suburbs.

The point to remember is that the issue is not nature versus nurture. It is the balance between nature and nurture. Genes do not make a person violent, fat, or a leader. Genes merely make proteins. The chemical effect of these proteins may make one's brain and body more receptive to certain environmental influences. But the extent of those influences will have as much to do with the outcomes as the genes themselves.

The confusion here is whether you can develop into a confident leader, not whether you're able to inspire confidence the day you were born. The ability to develop into a leader over time is what's innate. There is a starting point. The more 'lead' you possess from the beginning in the leadership virtues, the more opportunity you have to become a great leader. If you are challenged in one or more of those virtues, you will be disadvantaged, no matter what your environment.

> *The more 'lead' you possess from the beginning in the leadership virtues, the more opportunity you have to become a great leader.*

Conversely, a high disposition to leadership significance can be stifled if the environment is not conducive to nurturing those qualities. This is definitely true in home environments; and it also applies in the later settings in which we find ourselves either nurtured or demotivated to develop our leadership skills.

If you're born with raw leadership ability, your early experiences may serve to help you understand it, exercise it, come to terms with it, and 'fine tune' it. But your early experiences don't make you a leader; you are simply born with the predisposition.

> *Nature may be our internal guide (map), but nurture is our explorer and has the final say in what we do (destination).*

Still, to say that leadership simply boils down to "you have it or you don't" oversimplifies the matter. Usually, natural leadership is reinforced by parents, coaches, teachers, mentors or others who possess and/or value those tendencies.

Richard Arvey, Carlson School Professor of Human Resources and Industrial Relations and an adjunct faculty member at the University's Psychology Department, studied pairs of twins and the leadership roles they've held over the years to get the answer. Based on his research, he found that 30% of leadership is based on genetics, while 70% is dependent on environmental factors (Arvey, 2007).

Leadership is like poetry. You can improve language skills, build vocabulary, and learn about rhythm and rhyme. In that way one enables those inner poets to shine, *IF* there is a poet already inside.

Nature may be our internal guide (*map*), but nurture is our explorer and has the final say in what we do (*destination*).

Leadership…born? Or nurtured? Wisdom would seem to discount leaning toward either extreme. Ignoring the relevance of either would undermine our perspective and limit behavior. The filters through which we select and develop leadership need to be made through a bifocal lens.

DANGER: To embrace either extreme is to open the door to excuses for poor behavior and/or incompetency. We have heard them all.

> *"I can't help it, it was the way I was brought up."*

> *"He was raised in a poor environment. It's not his fault."*

> *"She was brought up in a dysfunctional family. No wonder she has such poor interpersonal skills."*

> *"It's just the way I am. Get over it!"*

As we search through the wisdom and experience related to optimizing our leadership potential, it becomes apparent that any formula for leading with vitality will take into account both nature and nurture. The significant leader will use personal awareness to develop a well-rounded set of skills and approaches that create an individualized formula for leadership success.

For You Leaders

We are who we are, but we can be more than we are today. We can be better leaders than we are today. We can make more of a difference in our organizations than we are making today.

How much it will take to change and how significantly we can make a difference will depend on virtues we naturally possess AND the environment we create to develop those qualities.

We now begin exploring the virtues of significant leadership. I invite you to be open to how much each of these reside in your life and in your leading. Which ones, if paid attention to and developed, could elevate your ability to be significant?

For You Seeking Leadership

For those of you who are in a position to identify, select, and promote leaders, begin creating the criteria you will use in your thinking and decision-making. Begin creating a model for significant leadership that you will use to compare candidates.

> *The filters through which we select and develop leadership need to be made through a bifocal lens.*

"**Leadership has to do with how people are. You don't teach people a different way of being, you create conditions so they can discover where their natural leadership comes from.**"

Peter Senge

What are those virtues we can look for within ourselves and others that will have the most impact on our leadership significance?

What will it take to be the leader you want to be and your organization needs for you to be?

Is there a formula for leadership success?

There is… and I call it

FORMULA

A Metaphor

The major organs of the body, including the brain, heart, lungs, and liver, which are the organizing and functioning centers of the body, require the fundamental elements of the body (such as amino acids, neurotransmitters, enzymes, hormones, and so on) for their life and functioning.

The *competencies* of leadership are like the organs of the body; and in our metaphor, the **virtues** for leadership significance are the fundamental elements necessary for leadership strength.

CHAPTER 4

COURAGE

> **Courage**: *mental or moral strength to venture, persevere, and withstand danger, fear, or difficulty. Implies firmness of mind and will in face of danger or extreme difficulty.*
>
> **Syn**: METTLE, SPIRIT, TENACITY, RESOLUTION.
>
> **Ant**: FEARFUL

"Courageous virtue is the essence of not just happiness, but life itself."

Aristotle

The Story of Ling

Once there was an Emperor in the Far East who was growing old and knew it was coming time to choose his successor. Instead of choosing one of his assistants or one of his own children, he decided to do something different. He called all the young people in the kingdom together one day and said, "It has come time for me to step down and to choose the next Emperor. I have decided to choose one of you."

The children were shocked! But the Emperor continued. "I am going to give each one of you a seed today. One seed. It is a very special seed. I want you to go home, plant the seed, water it, and come back here one year from today with what you have grown from this one seed. I will then judge the plants that you bring to me, and the one I choose will be the next Emperor of the kingdom!"

There was one boy named Ling who was there that day; and he, like the others, received a seed. He went home and excitedly told his mother the whole story. She helped him get a pot and some planting soil, and he planted the seed and watered it carefully. Every day he would water it and watch to see if it had grown.

After about three weeks, some of the other youths began to talk about their seeds and the plants that were beginning to grow. Ling kept going home and checking his seed, but nothing ever grew. Three weeks, four weeks, five weeks went by, still nothing had happened.

By now, others were talking about their plants; but Ling didn't have a plant, and he felt like a failure. Six months went by, and still nothing had grown in Ling's pot. He just knew he had killed his seed. Everyone else had trees and tall plants, but he had nothing. Ling didn't say anything to his friends, however. He just kept waiting for his seed to grow.

A year finally went by, and all the youths of the kingdom brought their plants to the Emperor for inspection. Ling told his mother that he wasn't going to take an empty pot. But she encouraged him to go, to take his pot, and to be honest about what happened. Ling felt sick to his stomach, but he trusted that his mother was right. He took his empty pot to the palace.

When Ling arrived, he was amazed at the variety of plants grown by all the other youths. They were beautiful, in all shapes and sizes. Ling put his empty pot on the floor, and many of the other kids laughed at him. A few felt sorry for him and just said, "Hey, nice try."

When the Emperor arrived, he surveyed the room and greeted the young people. Ling just tried to hide in the back.

"My, what great plants, trees and flowers you have grown," said the Emperor. "Today, one of you will be appointed the next Emperor!"

All of a sudden, the Emperor spotted Ling at the back of the room with his empty pot. He ordered his guards to bring the embarrassed young boy to the front. Ling was terrified. "The Emperor knows I'm a failure!" he thought. "Maybe he will have me killed!"

When Ling got to the front, the Emperor asked his name. "My name is Ling," he replied. All the kids laughed and made fun of him.

The Emperor asked everyone to quiet down. He looked at Ling, and then announced to the crowd, "Behold your new Emperor! His name is Ling!"

Ling couldn't believe it. Ling couldn't even grow his seed. How could he be the new Emperor?

Then the Emperor said, "One year ago today, I gave everyone here a seed. I told you to take the seed, plant it, water it, and bring it back to me today. But I gave you all boiled seeds which would not grow. All of you, except Ling, have brought me trees and plants and flowers. When you found that the seed would not grow, you substituted another seed for the one I gave you. Ling was the only one with the courage and honesty to bring me a pot with my seed in it. Therefore, he is the one who will be the new Emperor!"

Tiziana Ruff*

* Spiritual leaders of all traditions and faiths have in the past taught and learnt through examples like Christian and Sufi parables, Zen koans, Jewish Haggadah, Hindu legends, Native American stories and African fables. The messages that are conveyed transcend boundaries of religions, countries and cultures, and contain common elements. I will be occasionally drawing from these sources of insight that cross cultural boundaries in order to touch the threads that run through the tapestry of human wisdom.

Courage is the stuff that creates heroes from ordinary folk. Ling gives us that example. We can all recall other examples such as the legends from our childhood, including "The Sword in the Stone" and the Biblical tale of David and Goliath.

From fable to reality, how many times have we seen lack of courage be the downfall of many leaders?

Peter – a Story of Weakness

Peter put his hands around Steve's throat and squeezed. He tightened his grip with each attempt at escape. There would be no escape this time! There would be no avoiding the consequences for the horrible suffering Steve had put Peter through for the last twelve months. He took pleasure in watching the blood drain from Steve's face. As life slowly ebbed from Steve's body, he felt new life being poured into his. He counted the seconds before he would finally be free from his torment and his tormentor. If only he could make it look like an accident...

But of course he would never actually do anything physical like that. Peter knew that these intense moments of retribution fantasy provided needed therapy for the hours spent in frustration. The guy was driving him crazy.

His CFO, Steve, had to go. But Peter couldn't bring himself to fire a popular executive, even though he knew it was the right thing to do. The risks were too high and the personal consequences too scary.

Steve hadn't made any unethical decisions, at least none that he knew about. And Steve had not embezzled, at least nothing that had been discovered. He wished it would be that easy. No, the reason he should replace Steve was for not providing all necessary information in a timely fashion. It was Steve's seeming indifference, if not plain insubordination, that made Peter's blood boil.

Peter had all his rationalizations for 'why not' well thought out and rehearsed. If he did what he knew was the right thing to do, there would be an explosive reaction from the board. Steve had built strong relations with Board members because of successful audits. He solidified his value to the organization when he found a critical mistake made by the Controller that saved the company over three million dollars.

When Peter tried to plant the seeds of his intention to dismiss Steve with the Chair, his proposal met with a cold warning: 'You'd better know what you are doing.' Did he know what he was doing? It depended on the day, sometimes the hour, what the answer was.

If he removed Steve and hired a new CFO, he would lose members of his executive team. They loved Steve. Steve's sense of humor was legendary among them. They looked forward to the joke-of-the week more that Peter's opening comments at executive meetings. This wasn't funny. Peter was loosing the popularity contest.

Peter was tired of having this cloud hanging over his head, always questioning the consequences of his action, or inaction. He was tired of trying to satisfy everyone's expectations EXCEPT his own. His hesitancy extended to other areas of decision-making, causing frustrations among his team and questions of his competency.

Peter did not possess the courage of Ling. Instead, he settled for those morbid moments of fantasy. And it cost him. Eighteen months, six days and eight hours after he assumed the role of CEO, Peter was replaced by Steve. There was a board CEO confidence vote… and Peter lost.

What are you tolerating? What are you putting off, for whatever reason, that runs contrary to what you know you should be doing? Your answers may indicate to what degree courage is a virtue of your leadership. For the degree to which one is able to display courage will also be the degree to which one will be able to lead with significance.

"Courage is the ladder on which all other virtues mount."
Clare Booth Luce

I begin the exploration of the virtues for significant leadership with courage because it is the Achilles' heel for people who aspire to be significant and/or those who have expectations of significance. It is a quality that, if not innate, will be difficult to develop.

> *The degree to which one is able to display courage will also be the degree to which one will be able to lead with significance.*

As a leader, many times you face adversity alone. You can have all the typical buffers of degrees, title, and supporting cast members on your team; but when the call comes to be courageous, it comes to you alone. And in fact, too often, those you trusted to "have your back" (and your side and your front) suddenly are nowhere to be found. Having courage in the face of adversity is often a formidable task, because it is fear that we must face. And fear flies in the face of a deep human instinct – SURVIVAL.

FEAR OF FAILURE

Companies, organizations will give individuals the seeds of their future. There is optimism, hope, trust. There are good intentions. But along the way something happens. Leaders get scared!

It has been interesting, yet not surprising, that when I try to help leaders identify barriers to their success and use the 'f' word ("FEAR"), many quickly dismiss its existence. "I'm not afraid," they insist. "I have concerns," they spin.

While they may deny it, they all know it all too well. They know the feeling of *overestimating* the likelihood of something horrible happening and *underestimating* their ability to handle it.

Think about it. Here are highly successful people who have risen through the ranks of organizational structure to assume more responsibility than they ever have had before. They have received praise for their accomplishments and have been rewarded for their achievements. But alas, it is inevitable. At some point they will hit the wall of incompetency and be faced with another word – "FAILURE".

You and I have our limits. There is always a point when the requirements for the job exceed the knowledge and capabilities successfully utilized in the past. Often the doorway between competence and incompetence is passed through before the realization occurs. Cheering from the sidelines, momentum from past successes and the addiction to praise seduces us into believing there is no limit to our capabilities. But there is… there always is. That realization begins to creep into our consciousness in the dead of night. We are awakened from a sound sleep… in a cold sweat. It continues as more and more burning platforms occur and do not get resolved: criticism increases from stakeholders; achievements become more and more difficult… and denial no longer works. "Oh, my god," we hear ourselves whispering into the darkness. "When will I be found out?"

Having to face the board, or the annual stockholder meeting, all waiting for you to tell them what you have done for them lately, will you have the courage of Ling? Or would you choose behavior of the Emperor-wannabes? Recent history, sadly, too often gives us an answer.

Leadership will always *not meet* the expectations of some of its sponsors. The tenure of a leader in an organization will, in a large part, be determined by who and/or how many people you will disappoint. They hired you, or voted for you, or sanctioned you, or authorized you to do one thing… and now you are doing something else? You're challenging the status quo, pointing out contradictions between what people say they value and what they actually value. You are scaring people. They may want to get rid of you and find someone else who will do their bidding… and that can scare you! They will threaten you to get in line… or else. The more you resist, the higher the stakes will be.

> **"A man who wants to lead the orchestra must turn his back on the crowd."**
>
> *James Crook*

Make no mistake about it, the threat is real! You stand to lose a lot: reputation, security, power, control, status, resources, independence, identity, money, job. These threats will put you into a panic attack.

And in that state, you will be easily triggered into your 'dark side'. A brief comment by a coworker, the tone of voice from your spouse, an email from your boss, any small stimulus can set you off and make you crazy, or at least momentarily out of control. Your defense mechanisms kick in, generated by fear and fueled by adrenaline. Your bright, strategic, graceful, attentive self is no longer there, temporarily eclipsed by your more primal, defensive self.

Leaders get scared like normal people. They fear failure. They fear being found to be a fraud, an imposter (real or imagined). They fear losing relationships. Fear grabs you by the throat, choking the air out of your life - and all you want to do is to breathe... breathe at any cost.

The weak grasp at anything. They will fudge results, spin outcomes, play the blame game, all just to catch a breath of air... to live one more day on the job. And the more one lives in the lie, the more it can't be escaped. It gets exhausting to remember all the spins and lies; it becomes time consuming to keep from getting caught. One loses focus; one loses courage to do the right thing. Trust gets betrayed. And you have lost your will to lead!

> *Fear grabs you by the throat, choking the air out of your life - and all you want to do is to breathe... breathe at any cost.*

If you think I'm being melodramatic, you haven't sat at the pinnacle of an organizational chart, where the stakes are high, the air is thin, the buck stops on your shoulders, and you are alone... and afraid... and can't show it.

The Story of Hal

The company was in trouble. When Hal looked at the financials of their consulting firm, he found himself gasping for air, reaching for his medication at night. That collection of pill bottles had taken an increasingly larger space on his night table, and still, he couldn't sleep.

At the advisory board meeting six weeks earlier he had found a moment to confer with the Board Chair. His heart was beating rapidly. His hands were shaking with a perceptible tremor. "We're sinking," he admitted. "I bought into this company a year ago, investing all my life savings. I probably made the greatest mistake of my business life. Things are circling the drain, and I don't know how to stop it."

The Chair paused a moment. "Who is the strongest person on your staff? Who do you believe could lead this company into the future?"

Hal didn't have to hesitate. "Lauren," he said with confidence. "She has grown her division by leaps and bounds. To be honest, they are floating us right now. She is an incredible leader."

"Well," responded the Board Chair, "I think you've got your answer."

So, he had asked Lauren to come into the home office the following day, and over lunch, made her an offer. "Come into the home office," he said. "We need you here. We're in trouble, and I know that you can help us turn this around."

Her hesitation had troubled him. She looked him in the eye. "What about Dan and Lesley? You know that they will feel threatened by this." Lauren had, in fact, voiced her concerns about the productivity and commitment of these two key players in earlier discussions. "What will you do if they become upset and come to you?"

"I'll tell them to come directly to you," he replied. "Trust me. I'll have your back."

Three weeks later, Lauren came to him. "I keep looking at our financials, our immediate possibilities for revenue, and our trends. Our expenses far outweigh our income, particularly here in home office, where our income is decreasing for our services. Do you want me to wait, hold off before taking action? I have met with each of the staff individually, but the answers still appear the same." He knew that she was referring to layoffs. His heart beat faster. "No, don't wait. In fact, move faster." As she walked out, he felt sadness, yet relief.

Then, predictably, the others had trouped into his office. Dan and Lesley had come in separately, then together, bringing the administrative support staff with them. He was in the middle of a mutiny. He had to stop it.

Six weeks after it had begun, he called Lauren, who was attending a conference. "We need to meet when you get back here," he told her. Over another lunch, but this time with a different tone, he told her that he was pulling the plug, that she was no longer going to be leading the company. He was sending her back to her division.

With a stunned expression, she rebutted, "But you told me that you had my back, that you would stand by when the others came to you."

And in the end he did stand by, as he watched Lauren leave the company in which she had played such a significant role for over ten years. And he stood by as his two partners came into his office, closed the door, and announced that they were going to re-exert their control over the company. He did stand by.... even though his life savings was at stake.

Lack of courage prohibits facing the demons of fear. With courage those demons can be exorcized to the degree that they loose their control, their grip. And then the previously diverted energy can be redirected toward doing the right thing, doing what life is calling forth.

> **"Big goals can create a fear of failure. Lack of goals guarantees it."**
>
> *Unknown*

FEAR OF CHANGE

Another common source of fear is change. But leadership is all about change. Leadership is synonymous with change. And since change is the agenda of leadership, it runs contrary to our nature because you are wired NOT to change. Let's take a closer look at that hard-wiring.

Dostoevsky said that "taking a new step, uttering a new word" is what people fear most. For our prehistoric ancestors, change meant the prospect of starvation and death. Change also requires an expenditure of energy and time, and most of us don't feel that we have much of those to spare.

Think about Newton's first law—*a body at rest stays at rest, and a body in motion stays in motion.* The only way to change what we're currently doing is by adding a new force (typically in the form of an action), and we fear what this new force will cost us in terms of resources (time, energy, money). The thought of expending more energy or time runs against the survival instinct to conserve. Inertia feels much safer.

After we reach brain maturity (late teens, early twenties), our synapses have moved closer together and the intricate firing (off-on) among them requires minimal energy. We call the resulting behaviors, 'routines'.

Now, introduce change and the brain is commanded to create a new matrix of neurons that haven't been previously congregated in this formation. These new matrices haven't had the time and multiple firings of newly aligned synapses for them to be closely connected. Those new connections will require more energy when compared to old routines. Tilt! Messaging is broadcast to our system: *"Might not survive this new demand for energy!"* Instinct kicks in… resist… conserve… *"Don't do this!"*

It is the moment of truth. This is the moment that separates the men from the boys, the women from the girls, the leaders from managers. It is the moment that demands courage and defines leadership!

"Progress occurs when courageous, skillful leaders seize the opportunity to change things for the better."
Harry S. Truman

FEAR OF LOSING CONTROL

Studies have shown that uncertainty and situations which are viewed as uncontrollable arouse stress, like the situations in which we believe others are evaluating us. When we feel our understanding, control, or impact on events slipping away, we slide into a stress response. Our bodies, minds, and emotions lose resilience and creativity. We begin to see the world as more threatening. And a threatening world triggers that "f" word - *fear!*

There are many leadership books that prescribe the show-no-fear principle. But that is misguided advice. For one thing, while you might be able to put a smile on your face or can momentarily compartmentalize your emotional

You might be able to put a smile on your face or momentarily compartmentalize your emotional state, but you will never be able to stop your fear from being emitted.

state, you will never be able to stop your fear from being emitted. Just as with other animals, our fear can leave that 'scent' in the room (see box). That means when you walk into a room in the grip of fear there is nothing you can do to stop yourself from somehow communicating that emotion. Others get it, they feel it. They may not know WHAT they are feeling. They just know that they are feeling something from you, and that something is 'off;' and they respond to the feelings of wrongness. In turn, that encounter/relationship proceeds in an 'off' state that causes dysfunction, personal upsets, and interpersonal breakdowns… even when you have said nothing nor have done anything except enter the room. THEN, you add fear-triggered words or behavior; and then, unbeknownst to you, you have created an environment that sets the stage for, at best, poor performance, or, at worst, failure. You have, in fact, gotten what you feared! Productivity disintegrates. The more authority you have the more damage you will do when your fear controls you.

Don't try to hide it. You can't. By trying to hide it all what you do is create dissonance and conflicting messages. The words convey confidence, but the nonverbal messages convey fear. The only outcome in this situation is confusion, because people

> *The more authority you have, the more damage you will do when your fear controls you.*

believe more what they feel, rather than what they hear. Once you are triggered, you will trigger others around you. Fear begets fear!

If that isn't enough, while we are unconsciously creating a dysfunctional environment we have also created a filtering of external stimuli (actions/words) that we will interpret negatively. This simply enrages our fear and exacerbates our 'emitting' of dissonant messages, and we are caught in a downward spiral.

> *The following sidebar is not intended to bore you with technological jargon or intellectual highjacking. Rather, it is to legitimize the notion that when we do not master our psychology, in this case our fear, we seriously jeopardize our ability to function, threatening our physical and*

mental health. In other words, we give up our potential for significant leadership; and if we are in a leadership role, we amplify the collateral damage of our ineptitude.

The science is best summarized in Boyatzis and McKee's Resonant Leadership:

*"Stress arouses the sympathetic nervous system, which activates sets of hormones or endocrines. Once set, epinephrine and norepinephrine elevate blood pressure while blood is channeled primarily to the large muscle groups repairing the body for fighting or running away. It seems that the brain simultaneously shuts down nonessential neural circuits, meaning we are **less likely to be open, flexible, and creative.***

Other hormones are released that help fight off damage from inflammation, like swelling muscles. These hormones, called corticosteroids, have several damaging effects. First, they lead to a reduction in the healthy functioning of the body's immune system. Second, they inhibit creation of new neurons and appear to over-stimulate older neurons, causing shrinkage of the tissue. Under stress, not only does the brain shut down and lessen our ability to function, it also **loses the capability to learn.** As a result of this activity, we began to feel more anxious, nervous, stressed, or even depressed. In this agitated state, we have an increased tendency to feel we are losing control and to perceive things that people say or do as threatening or negative. We plunge into what neuroscientists call cognitive dysfunction. This can be magnified for leaders when on any given day they are faced with unrealistic demands, manipulation, and judgment."

> *Even with our intelligence and academic degrees and pedigree and charming personalities, we are fundamentally mammals with a survival instinct. And when threatened, we will do what it takes to survive.*

> "… the greater the anxiety we feel, the more impaired is the brain's cognitive efficiency. In this zone of mental misery, distracting thoughts hijack our attention and squeeze our cognitive resources. Because high anxiety shrinks the space available to our attention, it undermines our very capacity to take in new information, let alone generate fresh ideas. Near panic is the enemy of learning and creativity."

"Power does not corrupt. Fear corrupts… perhaps the fear of a loss of power."

John Steinbeck

Fear-driven tools can be recognized by: 'reasonableness', rationalization, deletion, distortion, generalization and emotional manipulation. Fear-driven leadership obliterates the heart and soul of an organization and drains the life out of those who work for it.

Even with our intelligence, academic degrees, pedigree and charming personalities, we are fundamentally mammals with a survival instinct. And when threatened, we will do what it takes to survive. There are typically three responses to threats (that produce fear). Superimposing some simple animal symbols will help distinguish among threat responses.

Fight, this is the *bull*, also known as the bully. When I'm confronted with a bully mentality… you know what I mean, the bravado, the aggressive in-your-face posturing… I wonder what is behind this protective façade of intimidation. What is the fear the bully is covering up? What is the person afraid of so much so that he or she is willing to destroy relationships to feel safe?

Flight, this is the *rabbit*. In the face of fear some can't get away quickly enough. They quit jobs, get divorced, stomp out of meetings, and worse, withdraw emotionally while remaining physically. One observes that they are present when, in fact, they have opted out and are, for all intensive purposes, absent.

Freeze, this is the *deer* in the headlights. In the face of fear, the meek will do nothing. They will neither fight nor flee. They will take no action. They will not take risk, and both growth and creativity may be casualties. Just as with our earlier business owner, Hal, such individuals become frozen in place. As much as they might want, they can't move, even when the headlights of a semi are coming right at them.

> **"Be not afraid of going slowly; be only afraid of standing still."**
>
> *Chinese Proverb*

Living in fear is not living; it is tantamount to being a prisoner of our own weaknesses, constantly awaiting the next injustice. Courage, on the other hand, decides quality-of-life in personal, as well as institutional, success.

Facing us is the river of fear made deep and wide by our hesitations, timidity, doubts, and paralysis. On the far bank of our lives resides our crises, bad hires, weak ethics, questionable acts, misreporting, anger, jealousy, regrets and the other results of character-challenged decision making. This is the stuff that demands dynamic and courageous leadership.

FINDING and KEEPING YOUR VOICE

> **"Courage is rightly esteemed the first of human qualities, because it is the quality that guarantees all others."**
>
> *Winston Churchill*

For leaders to be aligned with their high intentions, not only sustaining results but creating significance, finding and keeping your leadership voice is a fundamental necessity. Without doing this, you lead 'silently' and often poorly. No one wins in this scenario. Having your voice creates powerful, authentic dynamics where there is no limit to what you can achieve.

How do you and I develop courage? How do we courageously speak and act into the vacuums of fear, doing the right thing, living our core values? I don't believe we can become brave if we don't already have the predisposition. I do believe we can have more courage than we have had in the past.

My clients will tell me that after we meet they have more courage to do the right thing. All I really do is to help them get in touch with their "courage-within." Yet, I can't get them in touch with what doesn't already exist!

To offset fear, to supply that needed oxygen when gasping for air, some will create support systems (people – coaches, mentors, mental health professionals), routines (retreat or meditation) or destructive crutches (alcohol and drugs) to stimulate courageous nerve. Leaders can consciously choose to manage their fear.

Eleanor Roosevelt said, "You gain strength, courage, and confidence by every experience in which you really stop to look fear in the face."

The leader does not deny it, rather recognize when it is present and manages it, reframes it, and gets into action despite it.

Those who are predisposed with courage will more quickly get there and stay there, minimizing the impact of fear on themselves and others, minimizing the unintentional collateral damage fear can cause when unchecked. They recognize it, and stare it in the face.

To lead is to act. To have courage is to take charge, starting with one's own life. For the true hero is not the person who conquers others, but the one who conquers himself or herself first.

> *The true hero is not the person who conquers, but the one who conquers himself or herself first!*

To be courageous is to be prepared for the isolation of leadership.

"Courage is doing what you're afraid to do. There can be no courage unless you're scared."

Eddie Rickenbacker

Some selective wisdom...

- "Courage conquers all things." - *Ovid*

- "Courage is resistance to fear, mastery of fear, not absence of fear." -*Mark Twain*

- "One isn't necessarily born with courage, but one is born with potential. Without courage, we cannot practice any other virtue with consistency. We can't be kind, true, merciful, generous, or honest." -*Maya Angelou*

- "Our deepest fear is not that we are inadequate. Our deepest fear is that we are powerful beyond measure. It is our Light, not our Darkness, that most frightens us." - *Nelson Mandela*

- "Success is never final. Failure is never fatal. It is courage that counts."-*Unknown*

- "The only thing we have to fear is fear itself. Nameless, unreasoning, unjustified terror which paralyzes needed efforts to convert retreat into advance." -*Franklin D. Roosevelt*

- "The secret of Happiness is Freedom, and the secret of Freedom, Courage." -*Thucydides*

- "The leadership instinct you are born with is the backbone. You develop the funny bone and the wishbone that go with it." - *Elaine Agather*

What are you afraid of? Really afraid of?

Where is your source of strength?

Are you prepared to do what life is calling for?

COURAGE... is the first component, or virtue, of **Formula V.**

Formula

COURAGE

CHAPTER 5

HUMILITY

Humility: *not proud or haughty. Not arrogant or assertive. Reflecting, expressing, or offered in a spirit of deference. Free from vanity, egotism, boastfulness, or great pretensions.*

Syn: MODESTY

Ant: ARROGANT

"What a glorious revelation humility is of the human spirit... True humility is one of the most life-enhancing of all virtues. It does not mean undervaluing or underestimating yourself. It means valuing other people.... False humility is the pretense that one is small. True humility is the consciousness of standing in the presence of greatness."

Rabbi Jonathan Sacks

Some would argue that identifying humility as a quality for significant leadership is an oxymoron. After all, humility will be viewed as weakness in any social system that values status over substance, personality over character, and performance over depth. But humility as a leadership virtue has its roots in the philosophy and practice of the ancients.

In Greek and Roman cultures, leadership meant rank – position, not role. Leadership was a right attached by birth, marriage or adoption. Leadership did not depend on competence, gifts, intellect, or experience. Its purpose was to maintain the order of a highly stratified society.

Humility would not have been considered a quality of leadership in these cultures. Instead, there were four virtues that were supreme: courage, justice, self-control, and wisdom. Humility may possibly have been a virtue for a woman, but never for a man (Strom). And maybe not even for a woman, as we see in the ancient story of Athena.

Athena, goddess of wisdom, was a proud and talented young goddess. In times of peace, Athena taught Greeks about the arts. She herself was a skillful weaver and potter, and always took pride in her pupils' work, as long as they respected her.

One of Athena's pupils was a maiden whose name was Arachne. Arachne was a poor, simple girl who lived in the country. Her father was a quiet man of humble birth. He dyed sheep's wool to earn money for a living. Arachne wove beautiful fabrics of delicate designs, and people began to comment to her that surely she had been taught by the goddess Athena. Arachne denied this and stated that she was certainly better than Athena and that she had learned little or nothing from Athena's teachings. She even went as far as to say that she was a better weaver than Athena! Arachne was known to have said, "I have achieved this marvelous skill due to my own talent, hard work, and efforts."

Soon, Athena heard of the boastings of Arachne and decided to speak to her. Athena disguised herself as an old woman and went before Arachne, stating, "It is foolish to pretend that you are like one of the gods. You're simply a mortal whose talents pale in comparison to those of the goddess, Athena."

Arachne charged back to the old lady, "If Athena doesn't like my words, then let her show her skills in a weaving contest."

Suddenly, the disguise of the old woman was removed; there stood the radiant goddess Athena in front of Arachne. Athena accepted the challenge of a contest.

As the contest began, it was clear that Athena's and Arachne's tapestries were lovely. However, the goddess worked more quickly and skillfully. Arachne's attitude about her work showed that she felt her weaving was more lovely, but Athena felt it was an insult to the gods. This angered Arachne, especially since Athena requested an apology. Arachne refused, and Athena slapped Arachne in the face. Almost instantly, Arachne felt her head begin to shrink and her nimble fingers grow into long, thin legs.

"Vain girl, since you love to weave so very much, why don't you go and spin forever." Athena had turned Arachne into a spider.

So, it is said that all spiders have been punished for Arachne's boasting, since they are required to live within their own webs. Since those ancient times, spiders have been called arachnids.

(www.writespirit.com)

When have you seen leaders, challenged by this quality of humility, caught in their own webs of arrogance with its value of entitlement? They stand out in a crowd. Their larger-than-life heads fill the entryways. They will make sure you know how important they are while they also assure you of your place in the pecking order. There will be no doubt who is assuming the alpha-dog position in the pack.

John – A Story of Arrogance

"You're not listening to me, John."

There was that annoying whine he had been shutting out for years. It was something he had to put up with, but for which he had little patience. How could she have the gall to complain to him, when he had been supporting this family by himself for all these years? She couldn't handle a day without him.

But there it was again. His wife stood with her hands on her hips. "You're not listening to me. I am leaving you." That last sentence was a new twist on an old theme. Leaving? He put down the newspaper he was reading with his coffee.

He had heard that before; only the first time, four weeks ago, it wasn't his wife talking, it was three members of his executive team. Just last month he had surprisingly found their resignation letters on his desk.

The company was doing well - no, great! Even in the most challenging of economic conditions, stock value exceeded predictions, profit margins held, and there were even signs that they were making gains in market share.

John always knew that he had special gifts he readily offered to the company he loved. He appreciated the board having selected him as CEO, even though he knew he had earned that position. And he had the support of his executive team, members who were not as bright or insightful as he, but competent in doing their jobs under his mentorship.

That is why John was surprised to find the resignations of three of his top executive team members. Two of them gave a cryptic statement of 'pursuing other interests.' The third one, however, was a blatant tirade against his leadership and how he had mishandled the strategic vision of the organization. It further accused him of 'sitting on his throne of arrogance' while not respecting other leaders.

It wasn't long into the reading of that resignation that John became disinterested in what was being written. Instead, he began to get angry at the audacity of his Senior Vice President, whom he believed to be a friend. How could this man even suggest that he was at all responsible for the bumps along the road of success that the company had enjoyed under his leadership? And to think that there was a suggestion of disrespect, after all he had given them! His Senior VP insisted on competitive compensation and regular annual bonuses. In addition, the man had spent an inordinate amount of money on retreats, wining and dining spouses at expensive resorts.

It wasn't long before this ingratitude triggered an outrage that shook John to the core. He began to question the moral fiber of his Senior Vice President and the two manipulated clones. He wondered how the Vice President of Human Resources had blown their hires.

As John's administrative assistant entered the office bearing a number of documents for his signature, he began barking instructions to get the Chair on the phone and contact security to quickly escort the three traitors to their vehicles. In addition, he demanded a quick change of passwords and key codes for the three deserters. He wanted to get them out of the office and delete them from his life.

For the next few executive team meetings remnant members endured personal attacks from the still irate John, along with the questioning of values and morals against the three departed executives. Guised in his emotional rants was a threat that, if anyone else wanted to leave, he would see to it that they would never work again in the industry.

"You're not listening to me, John. I am leaving you. Maybe you don't care..."

At home, John finally got it right after his first marriage. He found someone who respected him and loved him for his superior intellect. And she was good arm candy at his numerous social events, not to mention her family connections in the business community. So he put up with her tirades. She was right. He wasn't listening, at least until she mentioned leaving... along with his two sons.

"You haven't been a father to your sons, nor a husband to me. That company of yours is your family, not us. It is not a coincidence that one of your sons has a drug problem and is failing nearly every subject in school, and the other won't even talk to you."

She was right. His family life wasn't great, but there had to be sacrifices for the sake of his success. Doesn't everyone sacrifice? But he had provided for them, given them everything they wanted. Took them on trips, bought them cars, paid their way through top colleges... and this was their gratitude?

It appears that the same script was being played out both at work and at home. It often does.

In his book *Good to Great*, researcher Jim Collins presents his analysis of companies that grew from "good to great" and <u>stayed there</u>. He found a quality in common among the leaders of these companies which had nothing to do with temperament:

"We were surprised, shocked really, to discover the type of leadership required for turning a good company into a great one.... Self-effacing, quiet, reserved, even shy- these leaders are a paradoxical blend of personal humility and professional will."

He adds, "[These] leaders channel their ego needs away from themselves and into the larger goal of building a great company. It's not that [these] leaders have no ego or self-interest. Indeed, they are incredibly ambitious-but their ambition is first and foremost for the institution, not themselves."

It is crucial that we not see humility as synonymous with being shy, withdrawn, quiet, self-effacing or self-critical. Humility is as much at home among the gregarious, ambitious and confident. Humility is not being negative about ourselves. Negativity poisons humility with self-pity and self-centeredness.

> *It is crucial that we not see humility as synonymous with being shy, withdrawn, quiet, self-effacing or self-critical. Humility is as much at home among the gregarious, ambitious and confident.*

Humility is not shaped by how we regard ourselves, but by how we regard others.

The argument for humility will mean little to those whose focus is on the short term and their own advancement. If the daily movement of the share price is our guide to significance, then we need not bother with humility. Arrogance, bravado, and a certain callousness in the use of people will get the necessary results... for as long as they last.

Those studying leadership might refer to this as the dark side of leadership, where leaders have a tendency towards narcissism, authoritarianism, Machiavellianism, and a high need for personal power. Do you have humility like the man who wrote the best-selling books, "Humility and How I Attained It" and "The Ten Most Humble Men in the World and How I Chose The Other Nine"?

"A frog in a well can only see the sky above him, and he thinks that small circle of blue sky is the whole world. He

believes he sees and understands the entire world = 'Frog-Well-Sky-World'."

Chinese Proverb

It is a proverb about the importance of humility. You are a frog in a well, and you can only see and understand what is available to you. Don't be so proud as to think you know everything. Peace comes when you realize that you don't understand it all, and you are not the center of the universe — even if you are the center of the well.

It is the height of arrogance (lack of humility) when leaders act out in isolation, believing that they know best. Flying solo is disrespectful and ignorant. It totally discounts the wisdom and experience of other individuals. If you are lucky, the decisions you make will be beneficial to the stakeholders. But in

> *Peace comes when you realize that you don't understand it all, and you are not the center of the universe — even if you are the center of the well.*

my experience, luck will run out sooner or later, and the consequences will be counterproductive, if not down right catastrophic.

In my work with leaders, it is not unusual for me to see arrogance as a façade that tries to hide fear. It is that best-defense-is-a-strong-offense strategy… the bully mentality. But that is not what I am talking about here. I am talking about a fundamental belief that one is superior… superior intellect, superior character, and the aura of "you should be honored to be in my presence."

It scares me when I see this narcissism in leaders. Such "me-first" thinking inhibits learning and improvement.

- Where is their propensity for growth and development? After all, they have already "arrived."

- Where is their ability to own mistakes, learn from them, and change? After all, it is always someone else's fault.

- Where is their ability to connect with people, enroll them, lead them? After all, they are in a different class.

How will anything be different than it is right now?

We get perceptions of people and situations that are made up of a few facts and a bunch of assessments/opinions accumulated over a lifetime. These 'perceptions' become our Truth from which we make decisions and act. We will get into arguments, hire and fire people, get divorced, go to war over our perceptions.

A person without humility will say, "So what?" A person with humility will consider that there might be other Truths to value. A leader with humility will become curious about those Truths, seeking their valuable nuggets in order to expand his or her own Truth, even changing his or her perceptions. This starts with not being the frog in the well!

> **"Greatness is not found in possessions, power, position, or prestige. It is discovered in goodness, humility, service, and character."**
>
> *William Arthur Ward*

St. Augustine once said, "It was pride that changed angels into devils; it is humility that makes men (*sic*) angels."

In the summer of 1986, two ships collided in the Black Sea off the coast of Russia. Hundreds of passengers died as they were hurled into the icy waters below. News of the disaster was further darkened when an investigation revealed the cause of the accident. It wasn't a technology problem like radar malfunction--or even thick fog. The cause was human stubbornness.

Each captain was aware of the other ship's presence nearby. Both could have steered clear, but according to news reports, neither captain wanted to give way to the other. Each was too proud to yield first. By the time they came to their senses, it was too late.

How much does this represent leadership we have witnessed in failed institutions? How often have you seen lack of humility ('a battle of egos') disrupt relationships and become a barrier to sustained results? How many times have these egotists caused tragedies that impacted human life?

I have worked for leaders who are like John. I have clients who represent his narcissistic personality. It is no fun. It takes a lot of energy, wasted energy, to maintain a constructive, productive, successful relationship, when you are dealing with another person whose idea of a perfect relationship is a relationship of one (himself). If you don't fit into his world, if you are not identified as valuable to his or her personal success, you will be ignored at best, if not publically shunned.

> *I have been in the presence of greatness; and what I am stunned by is the degree of humility that great leaders possess, and how that draws me into their presence.*

On the other hand, I have been in the presence of greatness; and what I am stunned by is the degree of humility that great leaders possess, and how that draws us into their presence. I will catch myself wanting to coach them not to be so humble, thinking they are too apologetic, that they may not fit my own (flawed) paradigm of leadership strength. I stop myself and remind myself of this wisdom from Lao-Tzu.

> **"I have three precious things which I hold fast. The first is gentleness; the second is frugality; the third is humility, which keeps me from putting myself before others. Be gentle and you can be bold; be frugal and you can be liberal; avoid putting yourself before others and you can become a leader among men."**
>
> *Lao-Tzu*

Others are drawn to the magnetic force which manifests itself around humble greatness. The walls of ego, superiority and patronization are non-existent. Others genuinely want to listen to their wisdom, follow their lead, not out of any fear or obligation, but out of respect and honor.

It's no secret. We live in a 'me', 'me', 'me' world. We want everything our own way, and we want it now. "It's my way or the highway," some say. People will see absolutely nothing wrong with this philosophy, protesting, "I have to have that philosophy, or I'll get run over in this rat race."

So, why would you want to be humble in this "me" world? Because it is a virtue of leading for significance. And it requires a mental shift, a shifting of self-talk, a change of attitude. I invite you to shift your perspective:

❑ From perceiving humility as letting people run all over you… to having the self-confidence to believe that you don't *need* to have everything your way.

❑ From perceiving humility as weakness… to realizing that your power is not derived from being always better than others.

❑ From perceiving humility as everyone looking down on you… to seeing that everyone will be drawn to your deflection of success onto them.

❑ From perceiving humility as meaning that you don't deserve anything… to experiencing a feeling of gratitude that recognizes that all successes and blessings are undeserved gifts.

❑ From thinking that "I will never get what I want if I'm humble" … to knowing that *"The only way to get what you want is to help other people get what they want"* (*Zig Zigler*).

❑ From feeling that "You can't be humble if you are a leader"… to understanding that "You will never be a leader if you are not humble."

In the *Art of Dreaming*, Don Juan tells Carlos Castaneda, "Most of our energy goes into upholding our importance… If we were capable of losing some of that importance, two extraordinary things happen to us. One, we would free our energy from trying to maintain the illusory idea of our grandeur; and two, we would provide ourselves with enough

energy to … catch a glimpse of the actual grandeur of the universe."
(Castaneda, 1993)

**On a scale from 1 to 10 (ten being highest).what number
would you assign to your degree of humility?**

The <u>true test</u> will be what others assess this number to be. The higher
the number you give yourself, the less likely you will ask others for their
assessment!

**Can you have lived alone, in isolation, and have achieved what you
have achieved?**

Who has contributed to your success and happiness?

> Combining **COURAGE** and **HUMILITY**, we create a
> juxtaposition of strength for a foundation to lead. These two
> virtues are essential in **FORMULA V.**

Formula

HUMILITY

COURAGE

CHAPTER 6

HONESTY

> **Honesty:** *a fairness and straightforwardness of conduct. Implies trustworthiness and incorruptibility to a degree that one is incapable of being false to a trust, responsibility, or pledge. Free from pretense or deceit. Transparent.*
>
> **Syn:** HONOR, INTEGRITY, AUTHENTICITY
>
> **Ant:** DECEPTION

This virtue has to do with honesty with your self and honesty with others about your self. Words and behavior are congruent. Authenticity is the outcome.

Wouldn't you love to have the same smarts, the same ability to assess hard problems and reach creative solutions, as many leaders you admire? Guess what: so would they! According to a new study in the Journal of Personality and Social Psychology there is more reason than ever to suspect that your leader may be faking it. "Fake it 'til you make it!"

Psychologists know that **one way to become a leader is to act like one**. Speak up, speak well, and offer lots of ideas, and people begin to do what you say… be influenced by what you want… and you can become a leader (*Kluger, 2009*).

They fake it… then they make it… and then they fail… and we wonder why? No need to wonder. They begin to believe they belong there, having the right stuff. They come to believe in their own deception.

Then, after having 'arrived', they find themselves having to defend against being found out to be a fraud. An attitude ensues, and the deception is perpetuated.

The Three Blind Men

Three blind men came across an elephant in the forest. As this familiar story goes, one reached out and caught the tail, one grabbed hold of a leg, and the third grabbed the elephant's trunk. The first man thought he was touching a vine, the second a tree trunk, and the third a large snake. The problem, of course, was that each had a limited perspective, and none could see how the parts were related to the whole. None of the three were being honest with themselves or with each other.

Where you stand on an issue depends on where you sit. People fix on particular positions, becoming adamant and zealous, to the point where arguments and disagreements lead to breakdowns in relationship. In our personal lives we get divorced, and in our societies we go to war by being obsessed with our perspective.

People have their own version of the truth. One of the truths about the metaphor of the blind men is that they are ALL blind. Isn't everyone? We may all think that we know the truth, when, in fact, we only know a piece of truth, with a whole bunch of personalized perceptions and assessments attached. While we may be blind to much of the reality of a situation, we think we are seeing the whole picture.

How many leaders do you know who operate out of this lack of self-awareness? How many leaders do not know what they do not know?

And because they "know," they don't ask. And because they don't ask, they miss opportunities to develop and grow, they isolate themselves and create a ceiling to their potential. The question becomes whether others in those leaders' circles actually see the world from the leaders' (limited) perspective, or if the followers simply "drink the Kool Aid," anointing the leader as all-

> *...because they "know," they don't ask. And because they don't ask, they miss opportunities to develop and grow, they isolate themselves, and create a ceiling to their potential.*

knowing and wise, promoting until the house of cards tumbles and the damage is painful.

Story of Mary

"There are a lot of stupid people in the world! And most of them seem to have ended up in my company. How else can you explain their irrational thinking and their constant resistance to everything I try to do? The problem is this stupidity seems to follow me everywhere I go, at least in the last three companies I joined. Each time I believed it would be different. And each time it wasn't. I feel like that damn ground hog. What's his name? Something-or-other Phil? I peek out of my hole-of-an-office and, seeing stupidity everywhere, retreat back for six more weeks, only to reappear to find that nothing has changed! Stupidity everywhere!" It is Mary's testimonial of her life.

Mary believes she knows, really KNOWS. Whenever someone tries to bring up a different perspective, she quickly shuts the conversation down by injecting her experience. Because she has "been there" (so she thinks), and she has experienced the same thing(so she thinks), she therefore knows (so she thinks). She is a guru in her own mind.

Not only does she disenfranchise all those around her, but what she thinks to be true, isn't. Truth is, Mary is another one of the blind who has experienced only one small part of the elephant. AND SHE DOESN'T KNOW IT! Or if she does, she is faking it to maintain the façade of authority; or she is hoping she gets it before she is found to not have it. Nevertheless, it is all a charade. It is dishonest.

Honesty is a quality of significant leadership that can open the door for learning and development. Conversely, lack of it – and in particular, lack of honesty with one's self - closes the door for learning and development. Dishonesty with oneself limits competency, and with such "blinders," prospective leaders may not be even capable of doing a credible job of "faking it 'til they make it." Like the classic example of the Emperor and his new/no clothes, everyone (but the oblivious leader) is privy to the leader's lack of attire.

Sterling – Story of Deception

No one bothered to tell Sterling that he was an arrogant jerk who routinely went into rants that got pointedly personal when things didn't go his way. No one mentioned to him how many nurses and technicians would manipulate their schedules to avoid being in the operating room when he was performing surgery. No one told him how under qualified he was for the executive leadership position he applied for and so greatly coveted. No one told him… until, finally, perhaps for the first time in his life, Sterling was denied something he really wanted – the position of System VP of Quality. No one told him until another embarrassing rant disrupted a board meeting.

Even then, after he was told that he had handicapped himself as a leader, that behavior that had here to fore been tolerated was not acceptable for a leader. Sterling's reaction? He went into a predictable rage, blaming his competitive physician colleagues and an overly politically sensitive administration. He felt betrayed and unfairly judged.

Sterling is a physician executive who is challenged by honesty. He is challenged to be honest with himself and, therefore, finds it next to impossible to be honest with others. He didn't "fake it 'til he made it." He never made it and didn't have a clue why.

Raised in an affluent family, possessed with above average intelligence, applauded when choosing medicine as a career, Sterling was routinely praised for accomplishments, rarely receiving negative or constructive feedback. He never believed it when he did. Believing his own "press releases," he went through his esteemed clinical career feeling exceptional and entitled until he was 'derailed' by the ignorant administrative board.

Sterling still practices medicine, but now, adding to his blindness, has an angry cynicism that fills the room wherever he goes, poisoning the environment. Just the kind of physician I want operating on me!

Psychologist and philosophers call it existential angst… not knowing who you are.

 I call it dishonesty: when looking into the mirror, not really seeing what you see, not believing what is looking back at you.

The facades we will be put up: the political games we will play, the bullying we will engage in, the one-upmanship we will routinely practice all contribute to this dishonesty. The problem with these attempts is they never work forever. They may work for a while; sooner or later the truth

> *Psychologists and philosophers call it existential angst… not knowing who you are. I call it dishonesty.*

becomes known, and the house of cards falls down abruptly. The leader may unfortunately keep the position, but the ability to lead has been permanently damaged, and the negative consequences begin to mount while the collateral damage spreads.

If you have experienced this situation, you know. It is an emotionally draining environment. It tests our resolve. It temps our own version of honesty, luring us to emulate the frauds around us. The outcomes, if we are lucky, may be good. But they are never great and certainly not significant.

Maturity – an Ingredient for Honesty

Honesty is a characteristic that requires maturity, persistence, an openness to risk and learning, particularly about oneself. It presupposes a level of humility and the attendant perspective that one can both "see" quite well, while also acknowledging that one may be blind to certain aspects.

Honesty, and the self-knowledge that comes with it, enables us to confront our self-deceptions. Life gives us the opportunity for an ongoing conversation with ourselves as we struggle with and can ultimately prevail in knowing our true selves. The growth that comes from knowing ourselves and continuing our "work in progress" throughout our lives can also draw others to us.

When we have this level of maturity, we cease having to defend ourselves and justify our behavior. We are at peace with ourselves, because we are aware of whom we are (and aren't), and are open to the countless opportunities to receive the gifts of wisdom and insight from those who are also blind, but may see differently and more clearly than we can.

Maturity starts with attitude. **Maturity starts with being honest with yourself.** In my experience with coaching, I have found that honesty is not typically learned later in life. It is more often innate in a person's personality or instilled at a very early age by a wise role model or cultural tenets.

Rarely, honesty can come from one's "falling from the pinnacle" or high point, a learning experience. If a person without honesty is fortunate, he or she may learn from a career or life catastrophe… but this is more rare. Behavior *can* be developed that weakens the deception and gives the appearance of openness. But in many of these cases, at the end of the day, the truth shows itself. The lack of true honesty and self-awareness may be revealed, particularly under stressful circumstances, destroying any trust that has been previously accrued. You can probably recall instances in which you have seen leaders with a tenuous grasp on honesty and self-awareness "show themselves" for who they really are, <u>after</u> the chips are down.

In our earlier example Sterling's dilemma was exacerbated by the environment in which he worked. There were many individuals who followed the same script and who were rarely honest with each other. Do you work within the same kind of environment? Do you go along with the script?

In such settings as Sterling's, and perhaps your own, accountability is rare, game-playing prevails, and trust can be non-existent as we watch the Emperor parade in his new clothes. What a sorry commentary this can be on absence of honesty. And if we aren't honest with ourselves and others, how honest will we be with customers, business partners, and other stakeholders?

If there were honest environments in the financial institutions and on Wall Street, would we have seen the same disastrous outcomes?

Honesty is the quality or condition of truthfulness with self and others, fairness in dealing, and the absence of fraud, deceit and dissembling. Nelson Mandela was recently interviewed and asked the question: "What was the #1 reason for your success - keeping sane while in prison, remaining humble as a leader?"

Mandela's answer was strong and unequivocal. He said, "The most important thing, much more important than anything else - is to be honest with yourself!"

Mandela went on to talk about the importance of knowing himself and the reality in which he existed. He was then able to live an act without illusions or fantasies. This reality helped him make wise decisions and kept him humble.

Principles of Honesty

There are two principles that guide honesty in leadership. The first is *intention;* that internal dialogue about who you are and who you are not; what you want to do and why you want to do it. It creates a resonate atmosphere around you where you connect with, inspire, and enroll others. Knowing that there were times when you did fake it, but it wasn't working for you, you knew that your behavior towards self and others was "off," insincere, awkward. You accepted what you didn't know and became intentional about closing the gaps in your leadership portfolio. There is truly power in clarity.

In ancient philosophy, Sufism teaches that if we are unclear or have doubts regarding the sincerity (honesty) of our actions, then we will be affected by criticism. Rather, we should be driven by sincerity of purpose (intention) without wasting energy on justifying and defending ourselves.

A second principle that guides honesty is **transparency**. Transparency is a state of mind. It is being open to what you are thinking and feeling... being transparent with what you know and don't know... being authentic... being comfortable in your own skin.

One of the defining characteristics of human nature is the ability to discern one's own faults, to be broken as a result of such faults, and in response, to seek a meaningful change. It is through this ongoing process of discovering our weaknesses and redesigning ourselves that we can grow. Socially, both forgiveness and the discipline process of reconciliation draw us into a crucible from which we can emerge more refined, more willing to see the heart of another, and more able to create just and lasting relationships (Ferch, 2004).

> *One of the defining characteristics of human nature is the ability to discern one's own faults, to be broken as a result of such faults, and in response, to seek a meaningful change.*

Are you more honest with others than yourself?

How well do others know you, really know you?

How well do you know yourself?

To COURAGE and HUMILITY, we now add our third virtue: HONESTY. We are progressing toward the leadership power of FORMULA V.

Formula

—— V ——

HONESTY V HUMILITY

COURAGE

CHAPTER 7

ALTRUISM

Altruism: *belief in acting for other's good. Assumes first and foremost a commitment to serve the needs of others.*

Syn: HARAMBEE, AGAPE

Ant: SELFISHNESS

"The leader leads through serving... And it has consistent and dependable integrity."

Max DePree

Harambee

In the Swahili culture there is the concept of *harambee* as it pertains to leadership. *Harambee* embodies and reflects the strong ancient value of mutual assistance, joint effort, mutual social responsibility, and community self-reliance. It is guided by the principle of collective good, rather than individual gain, through putting others' welfare and interest first.

In his book *The Servant*, James Hunter presents a powerful picture of what it really means to be this kind of servant leader, saying that leadership is ultimately rooted in our will. Hunter states that as leaders we can succeed not by forcing our will on others, but by demonstrating our will to serve. He distinguishes between leading through power and leading through authority. Many people can simply force people to do what they want, because they have the power to make them do their bidding. However, few people like to be forced to do anything. Eventually, such "power driven leadership" destroys relationships and, thus, one's ability to lead.

On the other hand, some have the ability to lead through authority. Authority is different than power. Power is something you have and can force on people. Authority is something you gain – it is given to you by the people you lead. How does one gain authority from those they lead? **Authority is gained only through service and sacrifice**, when people see that you have their best interests at heart. When they know how much you care, when they see you are willing to sacrifice and serve them, THEN they will be willing to follow. That's servant leadership. That is the significant virtue of altruism.

> *Authority is gained only through service and sacrifice, when people see that you have their best interests at heart, when they see you are willing to sacrifice and serve them.*

> **"To command is to serve, nothing more and nothing less."**
> *Andre Malraux*

The Cow and the Pig

There was once a man who was very rich and very miserly at the same time. The villagers disliked him intensely. One day he said to them, "Either you're jealous of me, or you don't understand my love of money - God alone knows. But you dislike me; that much I know. When I die, I won't take anything with me. I will leave it all for others. I will make a will, and I will give everything to charity. Then everyone will be happy."

Even then, people mocked and laughed at him. The rich man said to them, "What is the matter with you? Can't you wait a few years to see that my money will go to charity?"

The villagers didn't believe him. He said, "Do you think I'm immortal? I'll die like everyone else, and then my money will go to charities." He couldn't understand why they didn't believe him.

One day he went for a walk. All of a sudden it started raining heavily, so he took shelter under a tree. Under this tree he saw a pig and a cow. The pig and the cow entered into conversation, and the man overheard what they were saying.

The pig said to the cow, "How is it that everybody appreciates you and nobody appreciates me? When I die, I provide people with bacon, ham and sausage. People can also use my bristles. I give three or four things, whereas you give only one thing: milk. Why do people appreciate you all the time and not me?"

The cow said to the pig, "Look, I give them milk while I'm alive. They see that I am generous with what I have. But you don't give them anything while you're alive. Only after you're dead do you give ham, bacon and so forth. People don't believe in the future; they believe in the present. If you give while you are alive, people will appreciate you. It is quite simple."

From that moment on, the rich man gave all he had to the poor.

(Garden of the Soulby Sri Chinmoy)

The Sufis believe that giving is part of the law of nature. All of Creation is meant for use of itself in one way or another. The cow needs to give of its milk to produce more, the sheep needs to be sheared to produce more wool; and the same applies to human beings who need to give in order to achieve meaning and purpose in their lives.

The tree serves us by bearing fruit that can be picked and eaten, the clouds serve when they open up and provide rain, which is essential for the survival of crops and wild vegetation. The flower gives up its fragrance to everyone who walks by, and through its fragrance it will attract insects, which will pollinate it, enabling it to produce seeds and multiply. Service is inherent in nature (Azim, 2006).

To not serve goes against nature.

Stephen Covey had this perspective: "From an existential perspective, the raison d'être of organizations is to serve human needs. Really, there is no other reason for their existence. Individuals and organizations grow when they give themselves to others. Relationships improve when there is a focus on serving the other, be it at the level of the individual, the family, the organization, the community, the society or all of humanity."

Robert Greenleaf made popular the concept of "servant leader" in his writing during the 1970's. However, his tenets were not new, for the notion of leader as servant runs deep in wisdom literature crossing ethnic and cultural boundaries. The following is a sampling of its rich heritage.

Taoist

Templeton (1999) stated that, "Seeing Agape in the Tao is like trying to separate a wave from the ocean." The Taoist believes that leaders maintain a low profile, lead by example, and empower people through ownership of the task to do the work. "When the master governs, the people are hardly aware that he exists" (From the Te Cheng). The focus in the Tao of love and respect is in line with servant leadership.

Confucianism

Within the teachings of Confucius' The Analects, according to Yuan (2002), is the concept of jen that is summed up as "the humanity in humans, the benevolence or universal love." Jen includes the elements of "love, altruism, kindness, charity, compassion, goodness, perfect virtue, true selfhood, etc." This supports the idea that servant leadership fits well with Asian cultural beliefs.

Judaism

The Ten Commandments form the base of the Jewish faith and

are summed up in two statements: (a) loving God and (b) loving people. This sentiment can also be found in Leviticus 19:18: "but you shall love your neighbor as yourself." The Talmud, according to Lamm (2005), calls for all people to engage in kindness over charity. Kindness is an internal attitude referred to as chessed and means "giving of oneself to helping another without regard to compensation."

Islam

In the Mirrors for Princes (Muslim wisdom literature), guidance is provided for potential rulers. At the center of these guidelines is a deep admonition to serve the community and to eliminate human suffering.

Hinduism

Templeton (1999) pointed out that the Bhagavad-Gita teaches that those following the Hindu beliefs should be characterized by compassion and generosity, avoidance of immorality, the will to give, and the will to serve. According to the Hindu Times, Payal Agarwal (2005), a Hindu is advised to be caring, exercise authority with discretion, give the benefit of the doubt to employees, and build a group of caring and happy people. All of these items are in line with the tenets of servant leadership.

Buddhism

For Buddhists, the ego, and its attendant desires, are posited to be the fundamental causes of unhappiness. In this view attempts to satisfy the desires of the ego only lead to emotional suffering. In place of these the Buddha advocated selflessness, or no self (anatta). This is not the denial of the self, but rather the absence of essential distinctions between ourselves and everyone else. In this view, everyone and everything in the world is intimately interconnected in a set of endless causal networks. This interconnectedness is consistent with what it means to be a servant leader.

Servanthood is a universal ideal that runs deep in the cultural fabric of what it means to be a leader. IT IS RESONANCE IN ACTION!

Serving: A Contrary Ideal

And yet, being a servant is not what we have come to associate with leadership in the modern era, unless one means serving the wishes of the stockholders, stakeholders and otherwise those who wield power and influence over us. Still, the concept of service to others, and its importance in attaining leadership significance, has evolved, even if not widely embraced by all practitioners.

I don't quite understand this. Do you? When so many of the world's religions are aligned with this virtue of servanthood, but most leaders coming out of these traditions CHOOSE to behave differently, there is a reason. Is it a fundamental denial or rejection of those roots? Or perhaps might we be witnessing a shortage of courage, humility, honesty, or resonance? Or is it simply a matter of INTENTION and DISCIPLINE?

Patterson (2003) and Winston (2003) developed a two-part model of servant leadership in which servant leaders, through a construct called *agapao* love (a moral love toward followers), develop a sense of humility in working with other people and seek to behave for altruistic reasons, rather than for self-serving purposes. In addition, Patterson posited that from humility and altruism, servant leaders seek to understand the follower's vision or calling, and in the process of this build a sense of trust in the follower. Following the development of trust, the servant leader then empowers and serves the follower to achieve the follower's vision in the organization (Winston & Ryan, 2008).

Understanding the historical development of the concept of leader-as-servant, it is difficult to relate with our current real-world experience. It seems surreal in the world of business and high finance. This quality of significant leadership is the rarest of the five. Gandhi and Jesus Christ are often lifted up as great examples of servant-leadership. But these archetypes are rarely seen in our industrial leaders, even though we see glimpses of their *agape* in their philanthropy.

It is sad to observe, however, how few make serving a priority value, and how little in time and commitment is made beyond token gestures. Leaders from the business world who give of their power and wealth for the benefit of others, including Bill and Melinda Gates, appear to be the exception, rather than the norm. If I seem to be cynical, I am in this regard, as the relationship gap widens between leaders and followers, and the economic gap broadens between the haves and the have-nots.

To make matters worse, the very organizations who might support and influence this altruism virtue are mired deeply in their own hypocrisy. I find servant leadership too often missing in religious communities as religious leaders hide behind its emotional appeal and rhetoric to cover up greed, control, lust and zealotry.

As identified above, religions of the world share a common tenet of belief, but fail their constituencies when headlines recount abuses of power, corruption, and moral decadence. They then lose whatever influence or credibility they had in helping to define and instruct leadership with its ethical obligations. And yet, their responsibility to be the conscience of society, and the moral and ethical compass of leadership, remains in principle, if not in practice.

Can one teach servanthood? Can one be taught to consider first and foremost the needs of others, even when facing the pressure of the board to increase profits and market share? I wrestle with this one. Truly, it can occur, if one was raised in an environment where serving others was the norm, and behavior was modeled as members of the family lived their resolve. But beyond this influence, can one be a servant leader represented by the likes of Ghandi or Jesus Christ without being born with the predisposition to serve? Are we left with the prospect of having only a few born every century or so to bring their gifts of *agape*?

I believe that there are many more of us who have as part of their DNA the desire to serve as leaders. However, without the courage to stand up to the secular norm of survival-of-the-fittest, they may not seek out opportunities or will become discouraged with the conflict of serving in the face of gaining control, pleasing board members, and other forces within and outside the organization.

> **"One thing I know: the only ones among you who will be really happy are those who will have sought and found how to serve."**
>
> *Albert Schweitzer*

Story of Mark – A True Story

Mark inherited a mess. Financials were tanking, customers were bailing, and his executive team was defensive and walled within their own organizational silos. The corporate office was beginning to consider closing the operation. Installing Mark as leader was their last course of action before they pulled the plug.

One by one he replaced the executives and demanded accountability among the managers. Several unpopular reorganizations were carried out. After 18 months the division achieved solid ground and, in fact, began to lead the whole corporation in several metrics.

Mark had succeeded in performing up to his reputation as a "turn-around specialist." If I would ask you to describe this leader, what characteristics would you choose? Determined? Fearless? Ruthless? Focused? Heartless? What you wouldn't expect from a leader with this reputation and performance would be what happened next.

After his second year as CEO, Mark got a surprise from his board chair. It was a large bonus check. He hadn't expected it, because 1) while the organization had done well recently, it had not performed up to his expectations; and 2) "it was a team effort," he would quickly remark whenever praise was directed toward him. In fact, that is exactly what he said to his board chair when he was given the bonus. "I can't accept it, because it was a team effort," protested Mark, to the chair's shocked response.

But his board chair insisted that he accept the bonus. Mark thought a moment, then countered by suggesting that he distribute his bonus among his team who hadn't receive bonuses. They had voted to suspend their bonuses in order that employees at other levels in the organization would get some 'success-sharing.' At the next meeting of his team, he presented and divided the bonus which he had been given among the members of his team.

"The essence of leadership is not giving things or even providing visions. It is offering oneself and one's spirit.... When the spirit is right, gift giving transforms an organization from a place of work to a way of life."

Lee Bolman & Terrence Deal

A member of Mark's team was so moved by his generosity that she wrote, "It wasn't the money that moved me the most; it was his thinking about us and the resulting display of caring and love that he showed each of us."

"The true measure of a person is not how much he has accumulated during his lifetime, but rather, how much of himself he has given to others."

Ted Collins

What needs of people (in the world or your organization) do you see and have a passion for?

How are you willing to serve those needs?

What can you begin doing today?

They await your agape!

The fourth virtue, ALTUISM, joins COURAGE, HUMILITY, and HONESTY in the power of FORMULA V.

Formula

ALTRUISM

HONESTY   V   HUMILITY

COURAGE

CHAPTER 8

RESONANCE

> **Resonance:** The a*wareness of and sensitivity to the feelings of others, influencing behavior accordingly.*
>
> **Syn:** TIMBRE, SYNCHRONICITY, ATTUNEMENT, UBUNTU
>
> **Ant:** DISONNANCE

"You may be able to buy someone's hand and back, but you cannot buy his or her heart, mind and spirit."

Stephen Covey

Socially intelligent leadership starts with being fully present and getting in sync with others. Once a leader is engaged, then the full plethora of social intelligence can come into play, from sensing how people feel and why they feel as they do, to interacting smoothly enough to assist in moving people into a positive state.

Businesses are on the front lines of applying social intelligence, as Daniel Goleman writes in his sequel to *Emotional Intelligence* (Goleman, 1995). As people work longer and longer hours, businesses become their substitute family, community, and social networks. In this age of "employment at will," most of us can be tossed out at the will of management. That inherent threat means that in more and more organizations hope and fear run rampant.

Excellence in management of people cannot ignore these subterranean affective currents. They have real human consequences, and they matter for people's ability to perform at their best. And because emotions are so contagious, every leader at every level needs to remember he or she can make matters either worse or better (Goleman, 2006).

Across various cultures and belief systems, the message is the same:

> **"He alone knows Truth who realizes in his own soul are those of others, and in the soul of others, his own."**
> *Rabindranath Tagore*

Even more succinctly, we get this lesson summed up in an African Proverb: "a person is a person through other persons."

And we hear this message...

> **"All of the great leaders have one characteristic: it is the willingness to confront unequivocally the major anxiety of their people in their time. This, and not much else, is the essence of leadership."**
> *John Kenneth Galbraith*

If this is true, and history supports the premise, how can one know what the 'major anxiety' is? I suppose trusted advisors could tell a leader. I suppose a leader could perform research and study. However, unless one CONNECTS with people and "feels their pain," he or she will be unable to elevate awareness of others' emotions to prioritize and become motivated to 'confront unequivocally' that anxiety.

A connected leader was described this way: "He just knew. It wasn't so much he understood what he knew, he just knew, he felt it as surely as if it were hitting him in the face. It was real for him… it was on his radar…" That is resonance!

How many great leaders have come from the privileged classes who have unequivocally confronted the suffering of the underprivileged, the disenfranchised, and the shunned?

> *Unless one CONNECTS with people and "feels their pain," only then will a leader become motivated to confront unequivocally their anxiety.*

How would they know how others on "the other side of the tracks" feel? Why would they care? Are they possessed with a sensitivity that connects with the suffering no matter what their personal experience has been? Examples might include leaders such as Theodore Roosevelt, who came from a wealthy, privileged background, but who believed and acted strongly on behalf of socially and economically disadvantaged citizens before it was even fashionable to do so. He saw the pain and felt the need for change, despite his own world of privilege. That is resonance!

I don't believe this is a learned quality. I believe that people are born with varying degrees of resonance and to that degree will have the capability to be great… or significant. It is a matter of belief and thus attitude.

Does it mean one can't become more sensitive? Of course it doesn't. But the more one has to work at it, the more it will be obvious to others and come across as insincere, causing a disconnect.

It begins by <u>wanting</u> to resonate. That desire puts the agenda on your radar as you look for opportunities. The more you practice, the more it becomes a routine, the more it appears natural and authentic.

But those with the natural predisposition to resonate will easily and effortlessly leap over the chasms of differences, embracing the other and the other feeling embraced!

Ubuntu

In Southern-African Bantu language it means "humaneness – a pervasive spirit of caring and community, harmony, and hospitality, respect, and responsiveness—that individuals and groups display for one another."

Ubuntu inspires us to expose ourselves to others, to encounter the difference of their humanness so as to inform and enrich our own. Thus understood, the African proverb *"umuntungumuntungabantu"* translates as: "To be human is to affirm one's humanity by recognizing the humanity of others in its infinite variety of content and form."

Let's take a look at a couple of examples. Harking back to childhood, here is how this plays out on the playground.

On the Playground

Three twelve-year-olds were heading to a soccer field for gym class. Two athletic looking boys are walking behind, and snickering at, the third, a somewhat chubby classmate.

"So you're going to try to play soccer," one of the two says sarcastically to the third, his voice dripping with contempt.

It's a moment that, given the social code of these middle school boys, can easily escalate into a fight.

The chubby boy closes his eyes for a moment and takes a deep breath, steeling himself for the confrontation that lies ahead.

Then he turns to the other two and replies, in a calm, matter-of-fact voice, "Yeah, I'm going to try, but I'm not very good at it."

After a pause, he adds, "But I'm great at art. Show me anything, and I can draw it real good..."

Then, pointing to his antagonist, he says, "Now you, you are great at soccer, really fantastic! I'd like to be that good someday, but I'm just not. Maybe I can get a little better at it if I keep trying."

At that, the first boy, his disdain now oddly disarmed, says in a friendly tone, *"Well, you're not really that bad. Maybe I can show you a few things about how to play."*

Now, let's fast forward a few years. Here is how it plays out in the workplace.

We are about to listen in on a conversation between Chris, CEO and Matt, CFO. Matt has been underperforming recently, seemingly unable to make critical decisions, almost appearing to be frozen in place.

Chris - Story of Resonance

'Devastated' was the only word that came to mind when Matt and his wife were told that their seven-year-old daughter had been diagnosed with a rare blood disorder. The prognosis was bleak. There was going to be extensive, painful treatments over a two-year period with no guarantees of success. It was a parent's worst nightmare.

After only the first year of treatment, the cost of treatments exceeded the maximum on their health insurance. Matt sold his company stock, depleted their life savings, and was now getting ready to sell their home, downsizing to a smaller, cheaper place. Matt and his wife didn't know how much more they could endure. It seemed that each time they had reached their limit, they looked into the eyes of their daughter and saw her courage, and they rediscovered theirs.

The stress had taken its toll. Matt's performance had dropped at work. He knew it. Reports were late and contained mistakes, he seemed preoccupied at meetings and often unprepared for questions. He knew everyone was getting frustrated with him for not holding up his side of the bargain. While he liked Chris as a boss, there was only so much the organization would tolerate. He knew it was just a matter of time for him until he would lose his job. He wouldn't blame them. After all, he probably wouldn't have put up with himself for this long.

But he couldn't think about that now. He had to focus on taking care of his family, at any cost. Then he got the summons to Chris's office with no expressed purpose. It was a Friday… a bad sign because they typically axed people on Fridays.

It was true that Chris had been getting increased pressure from an increasing number of managers and executives, joining the board chair, calling for Matt's resignation. But Matt could not have anticipated in his wildest dreams what Chris had decided. Let's listen in on that Friday meeting.

Chris began, "Matt, I wanted to talk to you about your performance and what we have decided to do about it."

Matt tried to interrupt to say he fully understood Chris's position and was willing to accept the decision… but Chris pushed on.

"The board and I have agreed to put you on a three-month leave of absence with pay, beginning today. Your responsibilities will be handled by John during that period. I expect you to be on call to help him through the rough spots."

Matt didn't know what to say, but responded, "To be honest with you, I expected to get fired today. Why would you do this for me? I know the pressure you are under from the board, and doing this won't be popular with them."

Chris smiled and said, "I've built up some I-owe-you's on the board, and I called in one of the notes. You have been going through a lot at home, and it has impacted your work. We both know that you haven't acted like the man I promoted five years ago. And we all know the reasons for that. But it's not all altruism here. Frankly, it's either this, you resign, or we move you into a spot where your talents are wasted. I guess the worst move for everyone would be to let you go, and face a big severance package on our end, and a huge career setback on yours. Between you and me, we all value what you have brought to our company in the past... and what you could do in the future. I just want to give you an opportunity to get back to your old form."

"How could you know what we are going through at home?" he asked. "You don't have children. In fact, Chris, I know you haven't had to face any crisis

near the magnitude of what Sara and I have been through. You couldn't appreciate what we are enduring right now."

"You're right." Chris acknowledged. "I can't. And I don't know what you must be feeling. But what I do know is you are suffering deeply. I do know how much you need this job to pay for all of the medical expenses. You need the income so much, you are afraid to lose it, afraid to do anything to jeopardize the job. I know that the very thing you fear could very well happen unless something changes. I need you back in top form in six months. Let me know what else I can do for you and Sara. I will do whatever I can."

"I don't know what to say," Matt replied.

Chris nodded. "Just say 'thanks'... and go take care of your family."

(Epilogue: Matt took off three months due to his daughter's surgery schedule, returned to work in his 'old form,' and relieved to have gotten past the crisis. In fact, he was in better form from having gone through the experience and feeling the support and love from his boss. After five additional years, Matt succeeded Chris as CEO. A lot of Resonance and a dose of Courage saved a valuable employee and enriched the culture in which he worked.)

Both the example from the playground and the behind-the-boardroom scene offer a display of resonance, illustrating what Goldman calls 'social intelligence.' What could easily have led to a fight might now flower into a friendship. In the first vignette, the chubby artist held his own, not just in the turbulent social currents of middle school, but in a far more subtle struggle... in an invisible tug of war between the brains of the two boys.

By keeping cool, the aspiring artist resisted being pulled into anger by the others, and instead he brought the other boy into his own, more friendly emotional range. It's a display of the highest order of neural jujitsu, transforming the boys' shared emotional chemistry from a hostile arena to a positive one. The facility of our chubby hero showed a spark of sheer relationship brilliance (Goleman, 2006).

Chris, in our leadership example, could have taken the easier route and eliminated the problem. He would have quieted his detractors and put an end to his sleepless nights. However, to Chris it wasn't that easy. His rendition of social intelligence brought him close to another fellow human being, and he couldn't bring himself to coldly act. In the process, he not only saved a valuable employee, but reinforced the foundation for future success of the organization.

Resonance originates in the leader seeing people as people, not as simply another resource for deployment in support of the task.

Resonance also enables one to understand that people do things for their reasons, not for yours. Try as you might to get them to accept your reasons; but in the end, it will always be their reasons that provide the push forward. And great leaders know they can only achieve success through others. Great leaders connect with people and enroll them into common causes.

> **"Leadership should be born out of the understanding of the needs of those who would be affected by it."**
>
> *Marian Anderson*

Resonance bases its behavior on one of the governing values of ancient medicine: *"nihilnocere"* - 'not to harm.' Successful, significant leadership needs to be developed on principles such as this. The importance of resonance is highlighted by many others, across diverse cultures.

> **"The three C's of leadership are Consideration, Caring, and Courtesy."**
>
> *Brian Tracy*

> **"A marksman hits the target partly by pulling, partly by letting go. The boatman reaches the landing partly by pulling, partly by letting go."**
>
> *Egyptian Proverb*

Margaret J. Wheatley describes resonance a little differently in an interview. She describes it as love. "Even the best of leaders try to be objective rather than relational, and that's supposedly adding value to our work lives if we treat each other objectively. But it's again one of those huge things we get wrong. You can't lead without relationships, and you can't have relationships with one another if you have this curse of something called being objective, or one-size-fits-all, as a policy,.... We need to get away from the belief that you can run an organization using what we called objective measures or objective processes, which are actually just completely dehumanized. The fear of love in organizations is what makes your life as a leader far more complex. But it is also love that makes you much more effective" (Wheatley, 2005).

Peter Koestenbaum describes resonance as ethics. "Ethics, as a dominant leadership dimension, or strategy, means primarily that people matter to you.... Ethics also means that you know the power of love and that you act on that wisdom. Ethics means, furthermore, that you appreciate the personal enrichment that comes from being of service.... Ethics means that you can be, and are, interested in seeing the world from another person's point of view.... Ethics means that you understand the depth of a human being; you understand others as well as yourself.... Ethics means having the wisdom to be authentic, that is, yourself, in human relationships" (Koestenbaum, 2002).

Of relevance to our times, resonance is a concept that could revolutionize healthcare reform. It is preventative medicine. It is stress relief. In studies, caring relationships have been associated with lower blood pressure, enhanced immunity, and overall better health. Social networks and social capital have both been found to decrease mortality rates.

It is a win-win proposition. We connect, aligning our expectations, minimizing our misperceptions, maximizing our productivity... AND we get healthier.

Resonance is about trust.

You can trust that people are innately good and treat them accordingly; you can use trust to nurture the inherent goodness and divine spark in people.

> *It is a win-win proposition. We connect, aligning our expectations, minimizing our mis-perceptions, maximizing our productivity... AND we get healthier.*

The very act of trusting people unleashes a powerful force that empowers them and brings out the best in them. Trust, then, is recognition of the Divine in someone else. Ultimately, that is what you are trusting: there is a higher self. You do not trust their ego-centered self.

When you interact with people, you <u>choose</u> what level you want to interact on, and then choose what level to respond on. It is more about your being trusting than about the other person being trustworthy. When you initiate trusting energy and trusting behavior, it tends to bring out the trustworthy parts in the other person.

I have found that it is much more difficult to trust people when you feel little connection to them. A high RF (Resonant Factor) will foster trusting. Trusting builds bridges, and bridges build relationships… and relationships are what leaders influence.

PRINCIPLES FOR RESONANCE

- Everyone has his/her story. We may or may not know it. *Accept that reality, and be open to their uniqueness.*

- We have had similar experiences… we may have some empathy, but we have never completely had their life experiences or ability to know what or how they are feeling. *Attempt to walk in their shoes.*

- Everyone makes sense to him/her self, even when they make no sense to us. *Find out how they make sense to themselves.*

- No one possesses Truth. Each of us possesses parts of Truth. *Be a Seeker of the nuggets of Truth they possess.*

- Everyone carries a burden of fear (shadow), no matter how good they are of hiding it. *Give grace to them when they act out of fear.*

- Everyone is suffering and hurting to various degrees. You may not know what it is. *But you can feel their pain.*

*To what degree, and how frequently, do you put yourself into
the other person's position, walking in the other's moccasins?*

*When you are dealing with differences in content, style, and behavior,
how often do you view the other to be wrong... and you right?*

That degree and frequency will determine your Resonance Factor!

*How do you put yourself into a mental place
where you can be most resonant?*

We now have the five components of the formula
for leading with vitality: COURAGE, HUMILITY,
HONESTY, ALTUISM and RESONANCE. But
what forms the foundation for these virtues?

Formula

RESONANCE **V** ALTRUISM

HONESTY **V** HUMILITY

COURAGE

CHAPTER 9

SPIRITUALITY

The Heart and Soul of Significant Leadership

> **Spirituality:** *It is a sense of profound connection to things beyond and/or within one's self.* Intangible, life-affirming force that is present in all human beings. A *meaning system that has wide-ranging impact on how we think and act in everyday life.*
>
> **Ant:** NIHILISM

A root cause of leadership failure is the loss of connection with one's spirituality (and its requisite values and virtues).

This position can be easily supported by simply remembering what we have experienced in leaders: **nihilism** and **hubris**, these states of being, along with their companion narcissism, is the major contributor to leadership failure.

Nihilism involves accepting an inner emptiness as tolerable, even natural. This inner emptiness is then covered over with hyper excitation, thrills for the sake of thrills. It can be argued that it is because of nihilism that there is evil in the world, the cruel indifference to human suffering (*Koestenbaum, 2002*).

Professor Andre Delbecq at the University of Santa Clara first learned of the troubling, extensive state of executive hubris when, during a seminar attended by CEOs of 25 of the highest-performing firms on NASDAQ, he identified greed and hubris as the Achilles heel of big business. He largely indicated that temptation led many executives to feel as if they were all-powerful.

"We're very distressed by the fact that leaders try to distance themselves from the suffering the organization is going through, instead of being with that suffering," he said.

Explained Delbecq, "Successful leaders have to have a spirituality in order to avoid slipping into hubris and losing their moral compass."

Jim Collins, in **How the Mighty Fall,** identifies *hubris* as a leadership flaw that led to the decline of many an organization he studied. "We will encounter multiple forms of hubris in our journey through the stages of decline. We will see hubris in undisciplined leaps into areas where a company cannot become the best. We will see hubris in a company's pursuit of growth beyond what it can deliver with excellence. We will see hubris in bold, risky decisions that fly in the face of conflicting or negative evidence. We will see hubris in denying even the possibility that the enterprise could be at risk, imperiled by external threats or internal erosion. And we will encounter one of the most insidious forms of hubris: arrogant neglect."

Narcissism is the self-absorbed, conceited, egotistical belief that "I am the ruler of the universe...," "I have been gifted above all others...," "I am the chosen one..." For those who believe this way, their spirituality is skewed toward the notion that they have been called by a higher power to be in a position of leadership, and we should feel privileged to be in their presence.

Narcissists don't see themselves connected to anything or anyone except himself or herself, and they are fully protected by rationalizations that this should be so. They remain aloof, unaware, and unconcerned about why people react to them the way they do. And they are isolated, but they don't care; because in their perspective, it is the sacrifice one has to make for being elite.

> **Nihilism + Hubris = Narcissism = a mess!**

How did they get that way? We could argue that the cause is in poor upbringing or DNA (Chapter 3). Nihilism, hubris, and narcissism don't originate when one is appointed a leader for the first time. All that appointment does is to provide the power and environment for narcissism to grow and be expressed with an ever-expanding degree of horrible consequences.

In the forward to Mitroff and Denton's *A Spiritual Audit of Corporate America: A Hard Look at Spirituality, Religion and Values in the Workplace*, Warren Bennis states: "The authors demonstrate we are all on a spiritual quest for meaning and the underlying cause of organizational dysfunction, ineffectiveness, and all manner of human stress is the lack of a spiritual foundation in the workplace."

I propose that **leaders will lose their moral compass by losing contact with their spirituality.** AND they have been rewarded by their success, no matter how they achieved it. Such individuals do get results; and key stakeholders, particularly stockholders, often don't care whether a leader is liked or not. Nor do they often care about the suffering they have caused in the process. They do care about the benefit those leaders give. But is it a sustained benefit? Is it a significant benefit?

Leadership Nihilism

Even if we are fortunate enough not to experience nihilism firsthand in the workplace, you and I hear and read about it in stories that people tell about their experiences at work. Pain in these stories and the faces of those experiencing it is palpable as they share the experience of leadership nihilism.

You hear "stories of bosses who throw things at meetings, or storm out of them in a huff; stories of long-term employees being fired and given only a few minutes to clean out their desks – and that with an escort; stories of individuals being cut off at the knees in public, of executives holding staff up to public ridicule; stories of organizational leaders who manage by mood: charming one minute, demeaning the next; stories of executives who 'take no prisoners," who insist that is "my way or the highway"; stories of leaders who micromanage, who turn things over but never turn them loose" (Moxley, 2000).

These are the stories about leaders who are identified as the champions of industry, the saviors of corporate enterprise, who are lifted up as models in our business schools to be emulated because "they get results." They get results at any price; and the praise for their results reinforces their conduct. And they suck the energy out of people and ruin the environment of their organizations for creativity and change agility, not to mention sustained results.

Haven't we lost our way? Haven't we conveniently compartmentalized our connection with spirituality so we won't have to confront the demons within us? You know what I am talking about. Those demons can tempt us to behavior contrary to what is right; those demons can bring out the dark side in us, making us act in ways we are not proud of; those demons can cause us to betray the sacred trust placed in us. Without connection to our own spirituality, we can be driven, in large part, by nihilism and narcissism. We can experience disconnection with the spiritual belief set that grounds us and gives us purpose.

One of the ways we avoid connecting with our core is by not making distinctions between spirituality and religion. Haven't we too closely tied spirituality to religion? As tough-minded business people, we often relegate religion and its practice to the weak, in a quasi-chauvinistic mindset that sees religious practice as belonging "to women and children." Have we abdicated the discernment of our essence, our very being, to the priests and prophets of organized religion, draped in their rituals, obliged to sustain the status quo? Or have we simply lost our awareness of and connectivity to our core being, our spirituality, by choice?

Connecting Spiritual Values and Leadership Success

People commonly perceive that there is a conflict between the values and practices emphasized in spiritual teachings and those required for success in business leadership. Actually, research (Reave, 2005) shows instead that there is considerable agreement between the two.

Many experts expect strategy, intelligence, and even ruthlessness to be marks of a successful leader, but a review of the literature shows that these are not the defining elements. Instead, spiritual values such as integrity, honesty, and humility have been repeatedly found to be key elements of

> *Spiritual values such as integrity, honesty, and humility have been repeatedly found to be key elements of leadership success.*

leadership success. Personal integrity, for example, has been shown to be the most important element for engendering follower respect and trust.

"There is a clear consistency between the values and practices emphasized in many different spiritual teachings, and the values and practices of leaders who are able to successfully motivate followers, create a positive ethical climate, inspire trust, promote positive work relationships, and achieve organizational goals. These spiritual values and practices also allow leaders to achieve organizational goals such as increased productivity, lowered rates of turnover, greater sustainability, and improved employee health" (Reave, 2005).

IT IS A MATTER OF CHOICE. And with that choice comes an opportunity for leadership to move from good to great (Collins), from influence to significance (Kranzley).

Our choice gets complex if we aren't clear about the source of our spiritual virtues. This synergy between spiritual values and leadership practices can easily be dismissed when we mistakenly confuse organized religion and spirituality. Making a distinction between the two will help focus our consideration.

A brief review of world religions makes the point.

Islam

The building of community, concern for social justice within the organization and its vision, and equality of voice are basic themes of Islam. The values of service, surrendering self, truth, charity, humility, forgiveness, compassion, thankfulness, love, courage, faith, kindness, patience, and hope, in the workplace spirituality literature, are to be found not only in the Qur'an, but also in popular Islamic wisdom literature, philosophical debates and the mystical guidance of esoteric Islam, Sufism. Spirituality is an integral component of leadership in Islam (The Leadership Quarterly, 2005).

Buddhism

An examination of the Buddhist worldview as it informs leadership theory and practice would be incomplete without a discussion of what are called the four immeasurable states of mind. The four states, or Brahmaviharas, are love, compassion, joy, and equanimity. During the lifetime of the Buddha, those of the Brahmanic (Hindu) faith prayed that after death, they would go to Heaven to dwell eternally with Brahma, the universal God. One day a Brahman man asked the Buddha, "What can I do to be sure that I will be with Brahma after I die?" and the Buddha replied, "As Brahma is the source of Love, to dwell with him, you must practice the Brahmaviharas— love, compassion, joy, and equanimity"(Kriger and Seng, 2005).

Judaism

In the Judaic tradition, leadership is not primarily a question of having the right traits, competencies and behaviors for the situation, but a question of acting out of and being in touch with the source of meaning that the leadership is drawing its inspiration from and directing individuals in the community towards (Pava, 2003).

According to Judaism, human beings draw their being-ness from God, the ultimate source of meaning. One can pray without an object or action intended, to be simply in deep inner connection with the One Being or an aspect of the One Being such as love, truth, peace, or compassion.

Christianity

The Scripture is quite clear regarding character. Jesus shows his followers the nature of godly leadership. He takes off his garment and humbles himself like a servant and washes the feet of the disciples. Jesus told them that He was giving them a model of the kind of leadership He desired: Servant Leadership. Jesus talks of leaders with words like: Compassion, Humility, Gentleness, Generosity, Patience, and Service.

When the walk fell short of the talk, Jesus labeled the offenders "hypocrites." He denounced failed leadership as whitewashed sepulchers—tombs that were immaculate on the outside, but full of rot on the inside. It is the inside that matters to Jesus.

As Christians walk through life, they actively spread God's values through good examples, persuasion, and influence. Jesus called that being 'the salt of the earth', and the 'light of the world.'

When comparing the secular world view to the Christian view, one says "only the strong survive," while the other says, "the strong have the most to give." The secular view spotlights personal rights, the Christian view emphasizes personal responsibility. The secular view resorts to intimidation and power plays, the Christian view works through love.

It is true that all of these religions have, in differing periods in history, deviated from their espoused ideals. But these deviations need not be blamed on religion, but rather the leaders who have failed to embrace their spirituality.

It is not a matter of ignorance. It is a lack of awareness. It is focusing on what lies deep inside us, allowing it to come forth and influence our behavior. A couple of questions help surface this core.

- What is life calling for here?
- What is the right thing to do here?
- What would my spiritual models have me do here?

It is cutting through the static of the universe; the noise that which invades our lives daily; that interferes with our <u>being</u> the leader we want to be. It is seeing and feeling the suffering caused by the temptations of hubris and nihilism, and changing our behavior.

Spirited Leadership: Its Cross-Cultural Vocabulary

Consider these words that represent core principles of Spirituality and that can become the vocabulary of spirited leadership.

Nishkama Karma = selfless action without any expectation of fruits or results. A leader who behaves in accordance with this perspective is grounded in wisdom and in a state of equanimity.

The performer of *Nishkama Karma* is sensitive to the needs and values of those affected by behavior. He or she does not require courses in "stress management." This person follows his/her conscience, acts in accord with basic concepts of ethics in organizations, "walks the talk." The central practice of this tenet is *MINDFULNESS.*

Ahimsa (himsa) = "Do no harm" *(Nonviolence).* Ahimsa is a value in Hinduism, Buddhism and Christianity closely related to the concept of "unity." This "feeling of oneness … eliminates separative egoism (and) is the ultimate emotional foundation of non-violence." Non-violence here does not just mean physical violence, but also refers to nonviolence in thought, word and deed. The leader who is guided by the value of nonviolence performs his/her duties in peace, free from the demands of his/her lower self and its ego, and has a deep awareness of his (sic) connectivity to all living creatures, to all of existence. Nonviolence in thought, word and deed becomes a creed for the leader. A person with Ahimsa is acknowledged as a person of deep integrity, and obtains the respect and trust of not only his employees, but also of his customers and local society (Pruzan, 2001).

Ubuntu

Ubuntu (oo-BOON-too) = "I am because of who we all are." It is a word common to two indigenous South African languages, namely Zulu and Xhosa. *Ubuntu* is the essence of being human. It speaks about our interconnectedness. It is a belief in the centrality, sacredness, and foremost priority of the human being in all our conduct, throughout our life. When you have this quality, you are known for your generosity.

To be spiritual is seeing meaning in what we do, connecting with others in meaningful and selfless ways, and knowing that we are more than who we are.

Archbishop Desmond Tutu, Chair of the Truth and Reconciliation Commission of South Africa, stated it clearly, that in our experience, in our understanding, a person is a person through another. You can't be a solitary human being. We are all linked. We have this communal sense, and because of this deep sense of community, the harmony of the group is a prime attribute.

> **"Spirituality is knowing the true core of being within you, and realizing it is the same core within everyone."**
> *Peter and Kirsten Pruzan*

Does Spirituality enhance the work environment?

Spiritual resonance, as Diana Whitney describes spirituality in the workplace (Journal of Management, Spirituality & Religion, 2010), "carries with it a sense of the whole, a sense of the implicit interconnectedness and a sense of hope for the future based upon trust

> *To be spiritual is seeing meaning in what we do, connecting with others in meaningful and selfless ways, and knowing that we are more than who we are.*

in relational capabilities. Performance soars and endures in the presence of spiritual resonance. When people work from their strengths and seek to understand and support others working from their strengths, a seamless flow of activity and results occurs, and people consider themselves part of a unique and powerful 'we.' Spirituality resonance in organizations and communities creates an implicit safety net that invites creativity and innovation. It fosters high collaboration that is collaboration for the greater good, rather than simply collaboration to get the job done. It is a key success factor in an organization's capacity to balance the triple bottom line: people, profit and planet - and to be an agent of sustainable world benefit."

For many people, spirituality in the workplace is about energy. Spirit as Energy conversations are those in which people describe the feel of the place, the vibrations, the emotional tone, and what it evokes in them. The energy of the workplace may be positive, or it may be negative. The way people talk about their workplace not only describes the energy, it also creates it (Whitney, 1997).

Spirituality in the workplace places relationships at the center of the social organization. It not only honors all life, but also honors the whole and its collective wisdom. Compare this perspective with the isolation, narcissistic, or solo leadership model in many organizations today.

Globalization and diversity in the workplace create an imperative for leaders to: 1) connect with one's spirituality, 2) be influenced in thought and behavior by that spirituality, and 3) create the environment where others can be congruent with their own spirituality and that of others.

Spirituality is the development of trust. We trust people who operate in an ethical framework. Employees trust employers. Employers trust employees. And customers who trust a company will remain loyal customers longer.

There is beginning to be a consensus on which spiritual values are primary or core to an environment that is spiritually fed. The emerging consensus is summarized in the following list:

- Forgiveness
- Kindness
- Integrity
- Compassion/empathy
- Loving kindness
- Peacefulness
- Thankfulness
- Service to others

- Honesty/truthfulness
- Patience
- Courage/inner strength
- Trust
- Humility

- Guidance
- Joy
- Equanimity
- Stillness/inner peace

Pause for a moment to contemplate what your work environment would be like; how we would feel differently about our jobs; how we would act differently as leaders, if we only had a third of these qualities being the driving force behind our decisions and behavior. 'Transformation' would be too limiting a word, and 'Revolutionary' too political. 'Enlightened' would be too esoteric. 'Significant' is a word that comes to mind.

Leadership - Having, Doing or Being

One of the major challenges which many organizational leaders face today is the enactment of leadership with deep inner meaning for both themselves and others. This is related to the ontological level we form our worldview around. Stated simply, it is a question of whether leadership is based on having, doing, or being.

> *Deep inside, we know that and we find ourselves feeling unfulfilled, sad, or worse, indifferent.*

Having and doing are constructs which are familiar experientially to people in organizational settings. However, the direct experience and understanding of being has atrophied in the western world today, due largely to an overemphasis on observables. You know what I am talking about. They are those metrics you are being held accountable for, metrics that influence raises, bonuses, promotions and job security.

Essentially, if something is not directly observable or measurable, we as behavioral scientists, and those evaluating success, tend to question or deny its ontological status. "The facts speak for themselves," we dismissingly conclude. However, we still call ourselves, in English, human *beings*— not human doings or human havings (Benefiel, 2005).

The result is that we discount being a leader and instead focus on the numbers, thus putting a cap, a ceiling on our capabilities and success.

Remember what I said earlier. Given this limitation, we can still be 'successful,' BUT not to the degree we are capable of and not to the <u>significant</u> degree that sustains that success. And deep inside we know that, and we find ourselves feeling unfulfilled, discouraged, sad, or worse, indifferent.

What is it like BEING a leader, instead of simply doing leading? What would be different?

> **"Leading with soul returns us to ancient spiritual basics – reclaiming the enduring human capacity that gives our lives passion and purpose."**
> *Lee Bolman & Terrence Deal*

❑ There would be a constant awareness of what 'life is calling forth' and the routine searching for the evolution of that calling.

❑ There would be an alignment between your vision and behavior, with little hesitation or lack of courage for getting into action, because you know you are doing the right thing.

❑ A new level of energy would be found. Energy, once diverted and wasted, would now be focused with purpose.

❑ Peace would be discovered, that deep seeded calm when there would be synergy between who you are and how you are being for others and for the world.

❑ Limitless ability to influence, to lead, would be available, because others would connect with your authenticity as it resonates with theirs.

❑ And you would experience VITALITY!

Vitality: *exuberant mental vigor; capacity for the continuation of a meaningful or purposeful existence; power to live or grow.*

Syn: ENERGY, LIFE, STRENGTH

Ant: LETHARGY

Don't take my word for it. Listen to these testimonials.

Voices from Spirited Leaders

In 2002, Peter and Kirsten Pruzan began conducting interviews with business executives from North and South America, Africa, Asia, Australia and Europe. This resulted in their book *Leading with Wisdom* in which they report their learning about integrity and determination, courage and faith, humility. Here is a sampling of direct quotes from spiritually based leaders from across the world.

"I believe very strongly in the part of religion that says you should show love, kindness and compassion towards people and try to make a difference in the lives of those you touch. To me, if you are doing things that are not meant to further your personal interests, but which are meant to help others, then it is spiritual."

N. S. Raghavan
Joint Founder, Infosys, India

"If you are serving a purpose and you are doing it based on some fundamental values, and those values have to do with care and love, then you have great potential and you can be successful in almost anything."

Lars Kolind
Former CEO, Oticon, Denmark

"Spiritual resonance is in my view a very important aspect of good leadership and good teamwork. It permits the meshing of different personalities without jealousy or resentment. It permits one partner to cherish the limelight of the other partner. It permits listening even in the most difficult situations. It overcomes the dark shadow of the ego."

Ricardo B. Levy
Co-founder and Chair, Catalytica, Inc., USA

"Spirituality is that state of being what you were meant to be. Our self-worth comes in being who we are, not in doing what we do, not in achieving what we achieve, not in having what we have."

AnandPillai
Head of Centre for Leadership and
Management Excellence, HCL, India

"So is there a spiritual purpose in my life? No. Am I on a mission? No. I want to live my life with courage; I want to live my life with honor; I want to live my life with dignity, and I want to be harmless – not necessarily in that order. As a businessman, I live by the code, which some people call spirituality, which is to never hurt, steal or lie."

James Sincair
Chair and CEO, Tan Range Exploration,
Ltd, USA/Tanzania

"Spirituality to me is the application of the human values – truth, right conduct, peace, love and non-violence – in your way of doing things. But it's also more than that. It's trying to see God in everyone and trying to interact with everyone on a very loving basis, seeing everything as being perfect, and not pointing your finger at anyone or anything. Each of the human values that you are trying to live and put into practice comes out in reflections of what you are doing. Being spiritual is being humble and trying to help."

John R. Behner
Former Country Manager, Nabisco, El Salvador

"It's like the 'Hippocratic Oath' taken by doctors. It deals with not doing harm, making sure that when you leave the Earth it is not in a worse condition than when you got there, enabling future generations to live in similar if not better conditions. I am an ecologist. I don't think there are any hardcore ecologists who are not spiritual. Caring for the earth means not only caring for the environment; it also means caring for people.

It's a sense of responsibility. I am more pragmatic — more 'hands-on' spiritual — than transcendental."

Carol Franklin
Former World Wide Fund for Nature (WWF), Switzerland

"What comes to mind when I think about my overall spiritual perspective is a tapestry — a woven tapestry that has many threads weaving through it with a central thread that runs throughout. My spirituality feels like a beautiful, powerful central thread in this tapestry. Compassion, balance, grace and friendliness are words that ring as a spiritual theme for me.... Service is the cornerstone of this practice and I see my entire life as an offering to serve this sense of higher calling or purpose."

Amber Chand
Co-founder and VP of Vision, Eziba, USA

Life is calling for a paradigm shift in our thinking about leadership and the way we identify leaders. Competencies and skills all are tools one uses to achieve the outcomes we seek. But the qualities of courage, humbleness, honesty, resonance and altruism are the true measure of the kind of leaders we seek and seek to be. **And these virtues, when connected to our core being, open infinite possibilities for sustained success and a life that is significant.**

There has never been a time when humankind hasn't needed spirited leadership. Our times are not unique. But it feels unique because the consequences of failed leadership seem to have far greater, global impact than they might have in the past, damage that is deeper and more far-reaching, damage that creates permanent scares that disrespects life and undermines trust. Pick your crisis crying for significant leading. The choices are everywhere:

❑ Widening gap between the haves and the have-nots.
❑ Brutal consumption and depletion of natural resources.
❑ Dependency on oil and future energy sources.
❑ Bigotry and racism.

- ❑ Future nature of international order. Changing balance of political and military power.
- ❑ Changing economic and geopolitical balance.
- ❑ Climate change.
- ❑ Soil degradation.
- ❑ Fresh water shortage.
- ❑ Increasing power and influence of fanaticism.
- ❑ Dependency on global economy and politics.
- ❑ Health crises (HIV).

These are complicated and complex regional, national and global issues for all of us. To deal with them effectively, significantly, will require a special kind of leader; special kinds of leaders that will not let us repeat the mistakes of the past; **not let us get hijacked into decision-making gridlock resulting from hubris, narcissism, and nihilism.**

Closer to home, who will be making decisions on our behalf on these issues?

- ❑ In our **regional/state governments**, how will we distribute limited resources among people?
- ❑ In our **educational systems**, how will we educate our children to become global, responsible citizens?
- ❑ In our **religious institutions**, how will we influence the moral compass for society?
- ❑ In our **health care organizations**, how will we provide quality care for all people with restricted resources?
- ❑ In our **businesses and enterprises**, how will we grow and sustain success for the benefit of all stakeholders: investors, employees, customers, and the environment?

Who do we want to make the necessary decisions, globally and locally, on these critical issues? Based on recent history, I want a different kind of leader. I want a leader who is spirited (no matter how religiously supported). I want a leader overflowing with the virtues of *significant leadership.*

We all have countless opportunities to influence who those leaders will be. It isn't a matter of 'can we;' it is a matter of 'WILL WE.'

We have opportunities to be different in our leadership, expecting of ourselves demonstration of *significant leadership* with more courage, humility, honesty, altruism, and resonance.

> *If you are in a position of leadership, are you willing to consider changing how you are BEING a leader?*
>
> *What is life calling forth for you?*
>
> *What are you willing to do to become an authentic, spirited leader?*

Spirituality ignites the five virtues of COURAGE, HUMILITY, HONESTY, ALTUISM and RESONANCE into a life filled with Vitality. But what will it take to achieve this significantly?

RESONANCE V ALTRUISM

HONESTY HUMILITY

COURAGE

SPIRIT

CHAPTER 10

BEING A LEADER

The Structure for Making a Significant Difference

"In the tempestuous ocean of time and toil there are islands of stillness where we may enter a harbor and reclaim our dignity."

Abraham Heschel

We have heard the *cry in the wilderness* for spirited leadership; we have heard the call for leadership that is rooted with the five virtues of *courage, humility, honesty, altruism and resonance*.

We have explored whether or not these qualities of significant leadership are learned, concluding that greatness is a combination of both innate and developed qualities. We strongly advocate that even when 'greatness' might not be part of our equation, we all can be more, better, than we have been in the past, no matter what qualities have been part of our DNA.

Being versus Doing

We have distinguished between doing and being a leader. DOING leadership emphasizes individual-based knowledge, skills and abilities associated with a formal leadership role. In this paradigm we grow as leaders by acquiring knowledge and developing our skills through training, coaching, mentoring, and practicing our competencies.

In this context nearly all corporate training programs and books on leadership are grounded in the assumption that we should study the behaviors of those who have been successful and teach people to emulate them. But...

> **"... when leaders do their best work, they don't copy anyone. Instead, they draw on their own fundamental values and capabilities – operating in a frame of mind that is true to them..."**
>
> *Robert Quinn*

In fact, imitation often can be incongruent with natural strengths, and it can come across as inauthentic. Imitation without individualization can cause failure. Superficial imitation of others' strengths is as futile as attempting to emulate through wearing another's garments. What worked well in one situation and environment and for one interpersonal dynamic won't necessarily work in your current leadership context, either. To make the metamorphosis real, we must work from the inside out, not from the outside in.

BEING-centered leadership is engaged in a continual quest for greater awareness and consciousness. At a minimum this involves key spiritual practices, such as 1) knowing oneself; 2) respecting and honoring the beliefs of others; 3) being as trusting as one can be of others; and 4) maintaining a regular inner practice, such as meditation or constant prayer. It involves developing the interpersonal capability to build trust, respect, and ultimately, organizational commitment and performance.

BEING-centered leadership moves from being externally manipulated to being more internally directed. That means that we stop merely complying with others' expectations and conforming to current culture. There is no transformation in 'faking it until we make it.' The best one can expect from such mimicry is to create an inauthentic

> *BEING-centered leadership moves from being externally manipulated to being more internally directed.*

shell, through which others can transparently see. This may be why we see so many empty suits populating the corridors of our organizations.

To become more internally directed is to clarify our core values and increase our integrity, confidence, and authenticity (Quinn, 2005). Yet without projecting our values outward, we cannot shine our lanterns to lead; for it is in the context of others that leaders exist. In this world of significant leadership, we would look inward and ask ourselves: Who am I? And how can I *be my best for others?*

We conclude that connecting with our spirituality becomes a major agenda in our developing as leaders, increasing our competency and capacity to make a difference significantly, to let our lights shine.

> **"Leadership is not primarily a question of having the right traits, competencies and behaviors for the situation, but a question of acting out of and being in touch with the source of meaning that leadership is drawing its inspiration from."**
>
> *Moses Pava*

Spirituality is esoteric, not exoteric. It is not what is apparent, but what is hidden. It is not obvious, so it requires contemplation. The act of discernment will require different patterns of thinking and mental processing than the cognitive routines of envisioning and enrolling typically associated with leading. **It requires stepping outside the morass of everyday living in order to step inside the realm of meaning.**

Give Yourself a Timeout!

Before you go glassy-eyed on me, dismissing this as a dive into mysticism and the mysterious, I am talking simply about you giving yourself a 'time-out,' a time to connect with your core being.

"You do your best thinking by slowing down and concentrating." So says William Deresiewicz in an address to the plebe class at West Point. "You simply cannot do that (thinking for yourself) in bursts of 20 seconds at a time, constantly interrupted by Facebook messages or Twitter tweets, or fiddling with your iPod, or watching something on YouTube" (Deresiewicz, 2010).

In a world where many of us are rarely in the moment, where we allow ourselves to be distracted with the minutiae of instant messaging, texting, and information bombardment, we need to plan fully give ourselves a break to gaze inward. We need to break away from the call of the mundane, and search for the meaning that will lead us into significance.

What happens when we give our children a time-out as a disciplinary act? We force them to stop what they are doing. We put them in a different place (mentally, even physically) to contemplate. That is all I am suggesting that you do to connect with your spirituality. Because if we discipline ourselves to contemplate (no matter what form that takes), when we return to our work, our living, we will be in a better place, we will more strongly represent our core virtues, and we will have more power to lead significantly.

The Walnut – A Metaphor for Spirituality

The walnut has a shell, a seed, and the oil. The shell symbolizes the exoteric; the seed, the esoteric; and the oil, the essence that permeates the whole walnut; the essence that is inside and hidden (Jamal, 2006).

The greatest obstacle to BEING a leader, connecting with our spirituality, is an overemphasis on the thinking mind (*shell*), which results in thoughts and feelings becoming repetitive, routine. We then lose our creativity, our thinking-out-of-the-box, our limitless energy in favor of the more comfortable, safe, effortless routines involving intellect. This overemphasis distracts us and prevents us from assessing the inner stillness that is necessary for the deeper awareness of what makes up our core nature (*seed*), the energy (*oil*) to live and lead more fully, and the clarity for what life may be calling forth.

Make no mistake about it. The temptation is real; it is strong to remain in our comfort zone of intellectualizing and rationalizing, avoiding the deeper, richer, fuller domains occupied by our spirit. But the results of discernment and connection put us in a different place altogether, a place richly described by Jack Hawley.

Being in that Place- Our INTENTION

"This is the place of certainty, of moments of faith so high we merge with truth. This is where something at our core whispers "yes...yes" with full confidence. It brings the bounty of clarity, of seeing from higher self, the boon of being sure. ...Here repose moments of expanded capacity, instants of supreme quiet, brief periods of total acceptance, times of non-judging, wondrous intervals when we know we are doing exactly, precisely what we're supposed to be doing. These are the gift times of supreme congruence, when thoughts and intuitions align like iron filings under a magnet, flashes of perfect order" (Hawley, 1993).

How do we get there... to that place of 'supreme congruence' where we are confident, competent, and resonant?

> **"To make the right choices in life, you have to get in touch with your soul. To do this, you need to experience solitude, which most people are afraid of, because in the silence you hear the truth and know the solutions."**
>
> *Deepak Chopra*

SOLITUDE – The Structure for Significance

"Solitude is required for the unconscious to process and unravel problems. Others inspire us, information feeds us, practice improves our performance, but we need quiet time to figure things out, to emerge with new discoveries, to unearth original answers" (Buchholz, 1997).

It matters less HOW you create solitude in your life. What matters is that you first discipline yourself to experience it. What matters is that you put yourself in a position of discovery.

What I have found is when you put yourself in a 'position' to discover, it isn't you that discovers. What you seek discovers you. 'It' already is there. 'It' is already a part of you (again, recall the Walnut). When you put yourself in position, you simply become aware of what is. This is

> *What matters is that you put yourself in a position of discovery.*

what I mean by a different mental process, being open to being discovered! It is not an object to be found. It is not a problem to be solved. It is awareness of BEING, your being.

When we are in that 'place' of solitude, we learn to harness our power and focus on those things that will bring us to authenticity and wholeness. We begin to discover our voice. We begin to listen to that voice. We begin to express that voice.

It is then that we are able to change our perspective, step out of old ways of behaving, and live fully with *vitality*.

How do we begin to practice BEING a leader? It starts with paying attention.

Paying Attention - Heartfulness

Consciously being in touch with our inner strength starts with an awareness that we are more than the sum total of our thoughts, emotions, body sensations and overall mind content.

When we engage in a disciple of self-awareness and visioning we transform how we see things, and thus how we react to things and how we lead. Jon Kabat-zinn calls the outcome "heartfulness."

> *Connecting with our spirituality becomes a major agenda in our development as leaders, increasing our competency and capacity to make a difference significantly.*

"When we commit ourselves to paying attention in an open way, without falling prey to our own likes and dislikes, opinions and prejudices, projections and expectations, new possibilities open up and we have a chance to free ourselves from the straitjacket of unconsciousness…. So, mindfulness will not conflict with any beliefs or traditions – religious or for that matter scientific – nor is it trying to sell you anything, especially not a new belief system or ideology. It is simply a practical way to be more in touch with the fullness of your being through a systematic process of self-observation, self-inquiry, and mindful action." (Kabat-Zinn, 1994)

> **"Deeply connecting with one's spirituality and its related qualities often involves cultivation of inner practices such as contemplation, prayer, meditation, which serve to refine individual and social identity, so as to include the 'other'."**
>
> *Margaret Benefiel*

What I am proposing is not easy because it involves time. Time is a precious commodity for the leader. Everyone wants a piece of your time, and the waiting line is endless.

But this is time for your self that often, in my experience, is not a priority in the self-imposed martyrdom of the leader who is trying to meet expectations of all the stakeholders. This is a time for you to think, to tap the richness of your experience and wisdom.

This is important because we typically don't 'think' for ourselves, but rather, become inundated by others' thinking. You are marinating yourself in the conventional wisdom. In other people's reality: for others, not for yourself. You are creating a cacophony in which it is impossible to hear your own voice, whether it's yourself you're thinking about or anything else.

> *You are creating a cacophony in which it is impossible to hear your own voice.*

That's what Emerson meant when he said that, "He who should inspire and lead his race must be defended from traveling with the souls of other men, from living, breathing, reading, and writing in the daily, time-worn yoke of their opinions" (Deresiewicz, 2010).

The position of leader is a lonely one. It is intensely solitary. Regardless of the number of people you may consult, you are the one who has to make the hard decisions, the tough choices. You are the one who alone is accountable. At the end of the day, you are alone and only have yourself. It becomes extremely important that you are connected with that self.

Hold this thought. **This is the best use of your time AND, in the process, you will feel a freedom and peace you never thought possible.**

In the process (meditation) you will find a powerful relaxation response. It is a physical state of deep rest that counteracts the harmful effects of the fight-or-flight response, such as increased heart rate, blood pressure, and muscle tension. Molecular studies have shown that the calming response releases little "puffs" of nitric oxide, which has been linked to the production of such neurotransmitters as endorphins and dopamine. These chemicals enhance general feelings of well-being and make you more productive (Benson, 2005).

The journey, connecting with our spirituality, begins with you. To aid in the journey, every religious tradition has developed spiritual disciplines and routines. They include prayer, meditation, study, singing hymns, following prescribed rituals, retreating to sacred places, and contemplating nature. Not all these practices work in the same way for everyone. But the options are there from which to choose. All that is left for you is the *INTENTION AND THE DICIPLINE.*

THE STRUCTURE OF ONTOLOGICAL LEADERSHIP: Our DISCIPLINE

There are many practices to consider, but for the purpose of this writing, I have included three constructs or forms in which you can develop many disciplines. These structures are Silence, Meditation and Prayer.

SILENCE

Scientists hypothesize that if time travel were possible and we could go back 1000 years, one of the things that would shock us most would be the silence. Think about it. All the background noise of our modern world: television, cell phones,

We hear little of what we need to hear. The static blocks out the voice deep inside us all, the voice of our authenticity.

radios, cars, planes, furnaces, refrigerators...none existed a thousand years ago. Some even hypothesize that for the contemporary person, that silence would be deafening. Because we are surrounded by voices on TV, on the radio, on the Internet - all telling us what we need to know, how to get ahead, how to find happiness, and how to lead. The voices are many, and they are even conflicting. The 'noise' can be deafening. And we hear little of what we need to hear. The static blocks out the voice deep inside us all, the voice of our authenticity.

Deepak Chopra says that one way for us to discover our "essential nature" and "know who you really are" is to learn the practice of silence. "Practicing silence," he says, "means making a commitment to simply be," listening to what life has to say to us.

"Practicing silence means making a commitment to take a certain amount of time to simply *Be*. Experiencing silence means periodically withdrawing from the activity of speech. It also means periodically withdrawing from such activities as watching television, listening to the radio, or reading a book. If you never give yourself the opportunity to experience silence, this creates turbulence in your internal dialogue" (Chopra).

Silence can be a balm in the midst of chaos that often characterizes the life of a leader. This inner pulse will find its expression mostly when we are aware of its beat and give it freedom to be expressed. That takes intentionality. It takes silence to be able to listen for that pulse.

The Story of Ben the Ice Boy

*In a book called "**Directions**," James Hamilton writes:*

"Before refrigerators, people used ice houses to preserve their food. Ice houses had thick walls, no windows, and a tightly fitting door. In winter, when streams and lakes were frozen, large blocks of ice were cut, hauled to the ice houses, and covered with sawdust. Often the ice would last well into the summer.

One man lost a valuable watch while working in an ice house. He searched diligently for it, carefully raking through the sawdust, but didn't find it. His fellow workers also looked, but their efforts, too, proved futile. A small boy named Ben, who heard about the fruitless search, slipped into the ice house during the noon hour and soon emerged with the watch.

Amazed, the men asked him how he found it. (I closed the door), the boy replied, 'lay down in the sawdust, and kept very still. Soon I heard the watch ticking'" (James D. Hamilton).

What is ticking in your life that needs paying attention to?

Will you listen?

MEDITATION

We live in a culture where speed rules. I too often find myself in a hurry even if there is no reason. I am even in a hurry to rest! People get uptight today if they miss a revolution in a revolving door. We are an uptight generation of compulsive activists. There are ten times more things to do in a day than anyone can do, and so we feel we are always behind and failing to do all that we could. All we do is respond, respond, respond to stimuli. In such a state we are little more than reflex organisms.

We want peace, but it just does not fit into our schedule. Peace calls for doing nothing sometimes, and we can't handle that. Pascal, the great philosopher and scientist, said, "Most of man's troubles come from his inability to be still… Meditation is about 'stopping and being present, that is all.'"

Meditation is stopping, being still and paying attention, reflecting……..

It means learning how to get out of this fast current, sit by its bank and listen to the inner voice, learn from it, and then use our energies to guide us rather than tyrannize us.

"Meditation is more rightly thought of as a 'Way' than as a technique. It is a Way of being, a Way of living, a Way of

listening, a Way of walking along the path of life and being in harmony with things as they are."

Jon Kabat-Zinn

Greenleaf, the originator and proponent of the concept of 'servant leadership,' preferred to meditate. He even came to view it as one way of serving – meditation of one person enriched others, he thought. For Greenleaf, and others like him, it is after taking this inner journey alone that we are willing or able to actively engage the world, and to do so in a way that makes sense and provides meaning.

PRAYER

Prayer is a deliberate communication form that has many practices across all religions. Fundamentally, it is taking time to focus on the Other, to connect to a Higher Power or Presence. Prayer has many functions, but for our purpose here it is a structure for practicing BEING a leader. The underlying beliefs of prayer include:

- Prayer is intended to inculcate certain attitudes in the one who prays.
- Prayer is intended to affect the very fabric of reality as we perceive it.
- Prayer is a catalyst for change in one's self and/or one's circumstances.

Like Silence and Meditation, it is a psychological, emotional and mental 'time-out,' when we can step out, step back, and distance ourselves, to discern, contemplate, redirect, and commit.

CONNECTING - Opening Your Heart

When we fall into silence or meditation or prayer, we not only connect with ourselves, our spirituality, but we can also connect with others in ways that bridge differences and open possibilities.

> "Once I decided that the work was really how to keep my heart open, that led me to a number of practices beyond my own meditation, although some of the meditations I work with now are traditional practices to keep your heart open. One of the ones I've loved the most is to realize that when I'm suffering, whatever it is, whether it's anger, fear, feeling disconnected or treated rudely or whatever, to remember that the experience I've just had is an experience that millions of people around the world have, just by virtue of being human. If I'm sitting in a hotel room one night feeling lonely, just for a moment I might reflect that, "Just like me there are millions of people around the world feeling lonely at this very moment." This practice has been an extraordinary gift, of going from your personal experience outward to the human experience. Your own private experience is being felt by countless other human beings, and somehow this changes the experience from personal pain and anxiety to your heart opening to many others. And when I see someone else I think, "You're feeling just the way I do." That practice has opened my heart more than any other single practice and has made me feel part of the human experience and the human family" (Wheatley in *The Servant Leader*, 2004).

I began this writing by saying that it was SUFFERING that motivated me to attempt to reshape our thinking about leadership. It was the suffering of the victims of failed leadership and the suffering of leaders who haven't found their inner authentic power, who sit at the peak of organizational pyramids, gasping for a breath of fresh air.

I end this with the conviction that we can ease the suffering, and in some cases erase it altogether. But it requires us to make some choices.

We can choose to settle for mediocrity, falling prey to fear, feeling guilty that we are not what we can be and are not doing what life is calling forth. We can choose to turn the other way when leaders betray our trust, or settle for leaders who we suspect will be okay, even good, at best, but not great. We can choose to lower our expectations, being enablers of behaviors that have consequences that are unacceptable, yet which we accept.

OR, we can choose to tap into the courage within us. We can choose to be more honest with ourselves and authentic with others. We can choose to be humble, drawing people toward us. We can choose to be a servant leader in our giving, sending strong messages that 'I care.' And we can be resonant, be people who routinely look for understanding, walk in the other's moccasins, adapt our behavior accordingly. **We can choose to be significant!**

> *There is a river flowing very fast. It is so great and swift that there are those who will be afraid. They will try to hold on to the shore. They will feel they are being torn apart and they will suffer greatly. Know the river has its destination. The elders say we must let go of the shore, and push off into the river, keep our eyes open, and our head above the water. See who is in there with you and celebrate.*
> The Hopi Elders' Prophecy

It starts with each of us. We can begin to change how we are in our leadership. We can choose future leaders who bring vitality to our mission. Then, like the pebble dropped into calm waters, we will experience the ripple effects of our influence as it grows and spreads, being a gift to our organizations, to our relationships and to our world.

REFERENCES

The Arbinger Institute (Author) (2002). *Leadership and Self-Deception, Getting Out of the Box.* San Fransisco: Berrett-Koehler Publishers.

Arvey, Richard (2007). *Born to Lead?* www.carlsonschool.umn.edu.

Beazley Hamilton (1997). *Meaning and Measurement of Spirituality in Organizational Settings: Development of a Spirituality Assessment Scale.* Doctoral Dissertation: Washington DC: George Washington University.

Benefiel, Margaret (2005). *The Second Half of the Journey: Spiritual Leadership For Organizational Transformation.* The Leadership Quarterly, 16 723–747.

Benson, Hebert (2009). *The Relaxation Response."*www.suite101.com

Bolman, Lee. G., Terrence E. Deal (1995). *Leading with Soul, An Uncommon Journey of Spirit.* San Francisco: Jossey-Bass.

Boyatzis, Richard, McKee, Annie (2005). *Resonant Leadership.* Boston: Harvard Business School Press.

Buchholz, Ester (Jan. 1, 1998) *The Call of Solitude.* Psychology Today. www.psychologytoday.com

Castaneda, Carlos (1993). *The Art of Dreaming.* New York: Harper Perennial.

Chopra, Deepak (1994). *The Seven Spiritual Laws of Success, A Practical Guide To the Fulfillment of Your Dreams.* San Rafael: Amber-Allen.

Collins, Jim (2001). *Good to Great.* New York: Harper.

Collins, Jim (2009). *How the Mighty Fall and Why Some Companies Never Give In.* New York: HarperCollins Publishers.

Covey, Stephen R. (1990). *Principle-Centered Leadership.* New York: Summit Books.

Ferch, Shann R. (2004). Chapter *"Servant-Leadership, Forgiveness, and Social Justice"*, pg. 225, *Practicing Servant Leadership,* L. C. Spears and Michele Lawrence. San Francisco: Jossey-Bass.

Friedman, Edwin H. (1999). *A Failure of Nerve.* New York: Seabury Books.

Fry, Louis, Kriger, Mark (2009). *Towards a Theory of Being-Centered Leadership: Multiple Levels of Being as Context for Effective Leadership.* The Tavistock Institute. www.uk.sagepub.com

Gear, Michael, Gear, Kathleen O'Neal (2010). *Coming of the Storm.* New York: Gallery Books.

Goleman, Daniel (1995). *Emotional Intelligence.* New York: Bantam Books.

Goleman, Daniel (2006). *Social Intelligence: The New Science of Human Relationships*, New York: Bantam Books.

Goleman, Daniel, Boyatzis, Richard, McKee, Annie (2002). *Primal Leadership, Realizing the Power of Emotional Intelligence.* Boston: Harvard Business School Press.

Greenleaf, Robert K. (1977). *Servant Leadership, A Journey into the Nature of Legitimate Power & Greatness.* New York: Paulist Press.

Hawley, Jack (1993). *Reawakening The Spirit In Work.* San Francisco: Berrett-Koehler Publishers.

Heider, John (1985). *The Tao of Leadership.* Atlanta: Humanics New Age.

Heifetz, Ronald, Grashow, Alexander, Linsky, Marty (2009). *The Practice of Adaptive Leadership.* Boston: Harvard Business Press.

Houston, Paul D., Sokolow, Stephan L. (2006). *The Spiritual Dimension of Leadership, 8 Key Principles to Leading More Effectively.* Thousand Oaks: Corwin Press.

Jamal, Azim (2006). *The Corporate Sufi.* Fort Mumbai: Jaico Publishing House.

Kabat-zinn, Jon (1994). *Wherever You Go There You Are, Mindfulness Meditation in Everyday Life.* New York: Hyperion.

Kluger, Jeffrey (March 2, 2009). *Why Bosses Tend To Be Blowhards.* Time Magazine

Koestenbaum, Peter (2002). *Leadership, The Inner Side of Greatness A Philosophy for Leaders.* San Francisco: Jossey-Bass.

Lee, Gus (2006). *Courage: The Backbone of Leadership.* San Francisco: Jossey-Bass.

Lings, Martin (1977). *What Is Sufism?* Berkeley and Los Angeles: University of California Press.

Meaney, Michael J. (2001). *Maternal Care, Gene Expression, and the Transmission of Individual Differences in Stress Reactivity Across Generations.* Annual Review of Neuroscience 24: 1161-92.

Morrison, Mike (2007). *The Other Side of the Card Where Your Authentic Leadership Story Begins.* New York: McGraw-Hill.

Moxley, Russ S. (2000). *Leadership & Spirit, Breathing New Vitality and Energy into Individuals and Organizations.* Center For Creative Leadership. San Francisco: Jossey-Bass.

Pava, Moses (2003). *Leading With Meaning: Using Covenantal Leadership to Build a Better Organization.* New York: Palgrave MacMillan.

Pruzan, Peter (2001). *Blending the Best of the East and the West in Management Education.* Presentation at Management Centre for Human Values, Indian Institute of Management, Calcutta. www.iimcal.ac.in

Pruzan, Peter, Pruzan Mikkelsen, Kirsten (2007). *Leading with Wisdom.* Sheffield, UK: Greenleaf Publishing.

Reave, Laura (2005). *Spiritual Values and Practices Related To Leadership Effectiveness.* The Leadership Quarterly, 16, 655–687.

Sacks, Jonathan. *Humility, An Endangered Virtue.* www.jewish-holiday.com/humvirtue.html

Saul, John Ralston (2001). *On Equilibrium.* London: Penguin.

Schaefer, Chris, Darling, Jeri (1996). *Spirit Matters: Using Contemplative Disciplines in Work and Organizational Life.* Chestnut Ridge: High Tor Alliance.

Senge, Peter, Otto, C., Scharmer, Jaworrski, Joseph, Flowers, Betty Sue (2004). *Presence, An Exploration of Profound Change in People, Organizations, and Society.* New York: Doubleday.

Spears, Larry C., Lawrence, Michele Editors (2004). *Practicing Servant Leadership, Succeeding Through Trust, Bravery, and Forgiveness.* San Francisco: Jossey-Bass.

Strom, Mark (2003). *The Seven Heavenly Virtues of Leadership*. www.managementbooks.com

Wheatley, Margaret J. (2005). *Finding Our Way: Leadership For an Uncertain Time*. San Francisco: Berrett-Koehler Publishers, Inc.

Wheatley, Margaret J. (2010). *Perseverance*. San Francisco: Berrett-Koehler Publishers, Inc.

Whitney, Diana (1997). Spirituality as an Organizing Principle. *In the New Business of Business*. San Francisco: Berrett-Koehler.

Whitney, Diana (March 2010). *Appreciative Inquiry: Creating Spiritual Resonance in the Workplace*. Journal of Management, Spirituality and Religion, Volume 7, Number 1.

Winston, Bruce, Ryan, Barry (2008). *Servant Leadership as a Humane Orientation*. International Journal of Leadership Studies, Vol. 3 Issue. 2, 2008, pp. 212-222 . School of Global Leadership & Entrepreneurship, Regent University.

www.formulavleading.com